DSE (MR)
MANUAL

Teaching Pre-Vocational, Social and Recreational Skills

DSE (MR)
MANUAL

Teaching Pre-Vocational, Social and Recreational Skills

Edited by:
A. T. Thressia Kutty

Rehabilitation Council of India
in association with

KANISHKA PUBLISHERS, DISTRIBUTORS
NEW DELHI-110 002

KANISHKA PUBLISHERS, DISTRIBUTORS
4697/5-21A, Ansari Road, Daryaganj
New Delhi -110 002
Phones : 2327 0497, 2328 8285
Fax : 011-2328 8285
E-mail : kanishka_publishing@yahoo.co.in

Teaching Pre-Vocational Social and Recreational Skills
Edition: 2021

PRINTED IN INDIA

Published by Madan Sachdeva for Kanishka Publishers, Distributors, 4697/5-21A, Ansari Road, Daryaganj, New Delhi-110 002, Typeset by Sunshine Graphics, Delhi, and Printed at Rajdhani Printers, Delhi.

Foreword

"A book that fills the mind with beauty and opens the heart to what is lovely and lovable is a treasure forever". It allows transmission of knowledge from generation to generation and from place to place. Books have always been our best friend and a source of learning. We read and write for many purposes, most of the time they are either social or academic.

This manual attempts to serve the academic needs in the field of Special Education and Rehabilitation. Disability Studies are mostly dependent on western books and literature with very little being available within the cour.try. An effort has been made to fill in the gaps that existed, by preparing the manuals that would be simple in approach, easy to understand and serving the students needs. We hope that they will prove to be an effective tool not only for students and teachers, but also for parents, NGOs and organizations of persons with disability. The manual attempts to consciously follow the course syllabus and in the process explore the general and disability specific issues. In the process of creating such specifically tailored manuals for the courses, there are possibilities of oversights or errors despite our being careful. The Council would like to invite your suggestions and comments so that the subsequent editions, revised versions can be improved upon.

Time and again, it was emphasized that there is a great dearth of study material for the students as well as the teachers for the various diploma level courses in discipline of Special Education and Rehabilitation of the Council. This set the Council to take up the onerous task of manual preparation. Lots of effort has gone into the process, by the authors and the editors. Searching for the appropriate and relevant material that should go into the manual, readily understood by the trainee has been a gigantic responsibility executed with extreme care by the specialist team chosen for this purpose.

The Council would like to thank everyone associated with this project for their contribution. We hope that the manuals are able to unlock the doors of knowledge and successfully develop an insight into the world of persons with disability.

(Dr. J.P. Singh)
Member-Secretary

Contents

UNIT–1

Daily Living Skills Routine, Travel, Creative, Appropriate Interpersonal Relation–Employer/Co-worker, Job Related Behaviour–Punctuality, Regularity, Suitable Behaviour

STRUCTURE

- Introduction
- Objectives
- The Daily Living Skills
- Mobility and Independent Travel
- Teaching Daily Living Skills
- Maintaining Good Inter-personal Skills
- Job Related Behaviours
- Unit Summary
- Check Your Progress
- Assignment/ Activities
- Points for Discussion/ Clarification
- Reference

1

Daily Living Skills Routine, Travel, Creative, Appropriate Interpersonal Relation–Employer/Co-worker, Job Related Behaviour–Punctuality, Regularity, Suitable Behaviour

Introduction

The main objective of the paper XIV is to provide necessary knowledge, skills and experience for the students with mental retardation and additional disabilities at the transitional stage from school to work. The topics included in this paper are daily living, occupational, vocational, social and recreational skills. Activities of daily living are dealt in paper XIII. Therefore, the above-mentioned topics are dealt at the level of the students at transitional stage. This would help the special educator to include the job related skills such as daily living, social and recreational skills as a part of IEP at the pre-vocational stage.

The paper is written is such a way that the teacher trainees will be able to synchronize the practical paper "Work Education and Programming for Transition" with the theoretical aspects involved in it.

Objectives

After learning this unit the trainees will be able to:

- Identify the daily living skills to be taught to the students with mental retardation at pre-vocational level.
- Plan activities to train the daily living skills.
- Describe and teach job related skills to prepare the adolescents with mental retardation for suitable jobs.

The Daily Living Skills

Daily living skills are necessary for successful independent living and working in modern society. Acquisition of these skills can lead to vocational possibilities for students, depending on their particular abilities, interest and needs. Skills should be systematically included in daily classroom lessons rather than taught haphazardly or over looked entirely. Teachers many need to consider the individual's particular learning characteristics before they plan objectives, methods and evaluate the student's progress. These efforts will help teachers and learners to notice improvement in daily functions such as maintaining personal appearance, managing home and mobility in the community. The following daily living competencies help the students with mental retardation for a smooth transition from school to work.

1. Caring for personal needs.
2. Buying and preparing food.
3. Buying and caring for clothes.
4. Engaging in civic activities.
5. Utilizing recreation and leisure time.
6. Maintaining a home.
7. Getting around the community.

Caring for Personal Needs

Adequate hygiene, physical condition and health care are of special importance to the people with mental retardation. Parents and family members will probably help them how to take care of personal needs, but the teacher's involvement makes a difference.

(a) Dressing Appropriately

Social standards concerning the types of clothing, which are appropriate for different weather conditions, social settings and work situations are important skills to be taught. Teachers can use bulletin boards containing display that illustrates the major forms of dress. Role- playing technique also will be helpful to teach the adolescents.

(b) Exhibiting Proper Hygiene

As the students enter the pre-vocational stage they should demonstrate the ability to brush their teeth, wash their hands and face, use handkerchiefs, towels and napkins, and maintain a clean appearance. Adolescent/adult education should continue to help the students develop these abilities and expand their awareness of personal hygiene and grooming habits that are appropriate for males and females. This is one of the most important competencies since acceptance of an individual by peers, adults and employers usually based on personal appearance.

(c) *Demonstrating Skills for Physical Fitness, Nutrition and Weight Control*

The students sh7ould demonstrate knowledge of major body parts and perform exercise or activities that benefit development. As students develop fundamental knowledge of basic food items, nutrition, and weight control, teachers should seek cooperation of physical education and recreation professionals. Students can maintain their own health chart by recording height, weight, eating habits, games and sports.

Buying and Preparing Food

This competency relates to the purchase, preparation and consumption of food. In addition to the following sub-competencies the teacher should expand this area to meet the particular needs and abilities of their students.

(a) *Demonstrating Appropriate Eating Skills*

The students should be made aware of the meals time skills and demonstrate the ability whether it is in family or public situation. These skills should be taught in primary and secondary levels, reinforced in home and practiced in specifically designed field trips in the community.

(b) *Planning Balanced Diet*

After learning to eat properly students should learn to select appropriate food items for breakfast, lunch and dinner. Planning/selecting does not need to include actual preparation of a meal. They should learn the nutritional value and relationship between food, health and growth so that they can choose meals that provide the greatest benefits.

(c) Purchasing Food

Purchasing food is related to the sub-competency on making-wise expenditures and provide ample opportunity for teachers to train students in the use of measuring units of food and calculating cost. Students should be exposed to activities that will help them recognize differences on the quality and variety food items.

ACTIVITY

The teacher provides the class with a list of basic food items. The students check the prices at store and buys for the money, which they have.

(d) Preparing Meals

To prepare an entire meal the student will need to knowhow to use utensils, follow directions, identify various forms of measures, clean, cut and prepare food, and use devices for cooking. Every school curriculum should train the handicapped individual in the skills involved in managing the preparation of a meal. Teachers can certainly include parents in the instruction of buying and preparing food. Other objectives include preparation of meal according to directions and demonstrating kitchen safety measures.

(e) Cleaning Food Preparation Areas

This includes skills involved in the use of various cleaning measures, materials, disposal and removal of waste product and storage of utensils. Cleaning up is also an appropriate area for lessons emphasizing safety factors and measures involved in the entire preparation and clean-up process.

(f) Storing Food

This process requires that students learn how to store food and identify when food is spoiled. Teacher should demonstrate the techniques for storing food.

Buying and Caring for Clothes

Proper chance or modification of clothing can improve the handicapped individual's appearance and minimize the physical deficiencies he/she may have.

(a) Washing Clothes

When students begin to work their clothes, they will need instruction about the various laundry products and operating washing machine and dryers. These steps require cooperation from parents who in all practicality, are in a better position to evaluate these skills.

(b) Training and Storing Clothes

Teachers should provide instruction how to iron and store their clothing used during various occasions.

Each student should have a "repair kit". Parents and teachers should train them to use the kit to repair their clothing as per the ability level of the student.

(c) Performing Simple Mending

This includes matching thread colour, simple hand, sewing machine sewing and appropriate stitches for different types of tears.

(d) Purchasing Clothing

The students should be taught to select the clothes under the supervision of their parents for this, they should be aware of various colours, patterns and measurements.

Engaging in Civic Activities

General knowledge own country and own state and the names of the important personalities such as president, prime minister and chief minister should be imparted to the students. The purpose, need and the right for voting and procedures for voting also can be taught through various role-play and activities.

Utilizing Recreation and Leisure Time

This aspect is discussed in Part B, Unit 3.

Mobility and Independent Travel

The ability to travel is very important for person with mental retardation to commute between home and school, places of employment, recreation and health services. They should receive training for independent travel.

(a) Demonstrating Knowledge of Traffic Rules and Safety Practices

The basics of traffic rules, signs, symbols and sounds should be taught in simulated and actual situations. The teachers can use posters, field trips, and numerous audio-visual aids to emphasize the responsibilities of both pedestrians and motorists.

(b) Demonstrating Knowledge and Using Various Means of Transportation

Students should be acquired with specific forms of transportation that are available within the community. Teachers should construct activities that emphasize advantage and disadvantages of various forms of transportations. Finally students should use appropriate forms of transportation to reach school, work or recreational destination.

Teaching Daily Living Skills

The art of teaching has always required a certain amount of management. When the teacher prepares the individualized programme for the students, include the above-mentioned daily living skills. These skills are to be at a higher level, which would help the students to prepare themselves for a transition from school to work. In the primary and secondary stage, the teachers concentrate at lower level daily living skills. At prevocational level, as a part of vocational education, these skills can be included as perquisite skills and readiness skills to enter into the next important stage.

Maintaining Good Inter-personal Skills

It is a skill that interacts with the individual's feelings of confidence and independence and is a key to successful career functioning. Practice is the most crucial element of these competencies for teachers, parents and students. The students with Mental Retardation need the opportunities to exhibit the expected behaviours and responses for such everyday events as listening to another persons, asking questions, providing information, telling a story and expressing emotion.

(a) Demonstrating How to Listen and Respond

Communication depends upon the correct interchange of ideas or objects between people. The teacher should develop several abilities so students can complete this competency. They should be able to attend to the message by using all senses, develop adequate means of response, such as speaking, signing and writing to determine the appropriate meaning of the verbal or non-verbal message.

(b) *Make and Maintain Friendships*

Who is a friend? What do students want in a friendship? What can offer as a friend to someone else? What happens when a friend leaves?

Activity Tips

1. A class member has been invited for a party. Rehearse the expected behaviours in a simulated situation in the class.
2. Initiate a discussion on friendship...... Ask the students to tell the name of one of the friends. Why he/she likes him/her? What way the friend helps the student? In what ways the student shows his concern?

Let them understand that how to make friends and keep them is unique to each person.

(c) *Maintaining Appropriate Heterosexual Relationship*

When the students are in the company of students with both the sex together, they should be taught how to maintain their relationship. They should also be aware of the norms of the society.

(d) *Differentiate Between Relationships*

The skills for developing relationship at various levels can be nurtured by the family. Children learn about personal reactions and respect by observing their parents and by interacting with brothers, sisters or relatives. They may have already developed relationships of varying intensives with family members, neighbours, playmates and teachers. The teacher can begin with exercises that help students identify the different types of relationships that already exist or can be observed in the family and community.

(e) *Understanding the Impact of Behaviours in Others*

Our lives involve a mixture of relationships from dependence, through independence, to inter-dependence. The goal of personal independence involves the student's awareness of those behaviours that promote acceptance or rejection within the society. This anticipation influences interaction within a family, social or employment setting. Teachers and parents want students to understand and to foresee the effect that their conduct will have on other individuals.

Teachers at the primary level can begin with simple exercises inwhich students identify the way one person's behaviour produces other person's response. In higher classes, gradually the teacher can elicit responses for a given behaviour.

Job Related Behaviours

School personnel should emphasize the necessity of developing the work habits and behaviours that all students will need when they began responsible job. At certain times, teachers may simulate working environment in the school setting to illustrate the kinds of expectations employers have of competent workers. Field trips and parents can play an important role in developing job related behaviours.

(a) Following Directions

Employers expect their employees to follow directions accurately. These may be given either verbally or in writing and will range from very simple one-step to complex several steps. These directions should be remembered by the employees and complete the tasks.

How to Train

Games and role-play techniques can be effective in helping students develop these skills.

(b) Working with Others

The inability to get along with co-workers and supervisors is one of the most common reasons people fail on their jobs. Students must learn work expectations, and the school can become a fertile ground for teaching these interactive and cooperative skills.

- Teachers should create an environment that promotes development of these work skills by encouraging students to practice interacting and cooperating with others.

- Field trip and role-playing an be used to stimulate discussion on reasons for working with others and the need for cooperation.
- The teacher can simulate actual work limits where the students need to interact and cooperate.

(c) *Working a Satisfactory Rate*

The students should learn how to do work correctly at a sufficient speed. They should be taught to complete certain work activities within a specific period of time so that they form the habit as well as learn the concept.Time standards can be established for various work tasks in and out of the school.Teachers should check the student's progress until he/she meets the criterion.

(d) *Accepting Supervision*

Supervision can range from indirect to direct and infrequent to very frequent. Supervision can be constructive and critical. It is important for the student to understand the various forms of supervision and how they should react to supervision under different condition.

(e) *Recognizing the Importance and Attendance and Punctually*

The students should learn why attendance and punctuality are important to employer. (Loss of production, income, difficulty to finish the product on time.)

This can be taught in classroom situation itself by giving punching card. Enter the attendance and let the students understand the meaning of absenteeism. By sending the students for various activities and noting the time and dead line would help the students to understand the concept of punctuality and deadline.

If the student is absent or late, the need to take appropriate action also should be known to them.

(f) *Meeting Demand for Quality Work*

Students will need to learn about quality standards for various types of jobs. They should meet such standards on work assignments.

- Demonstrate the steps in completing a job and present a model of product with expected quality.

- Let the student learn to do and compare the quality with the model product. Let student continue to do till he/she achieves the expected quality.

  Example: Cleaning, packing and setting dining table etc.

(g) Developing Occupational Safety Skills

Many employers are afraid to employ persons with mental retardation because they believe that these individuals will have more accidents. Therefore, it is important to give emphasis in training occupational safety skills. Before placing on a job, analyze the job site and study the environment. As a precaution, prepare the student to handle the hazardous situations in the given environment and job site. Refer the topic first aid for more information.

Unit Summary

Acquisition of daily living skills can lead to vocational possibilities for students depending on their abilities, interest and needs.

The following daily living competencies help the students with mental retardation for a smooth transition from school to work:

- Caring for personal needs
- Buying and caring for cloths
- Buying and preparing food
- Maintaining a home
- Utilizing recreation and leisure time
- Getting around the community
- Engaging in civic activities.

When the teacher prepares the individualised education programme for the students, include the above-mentioned daily living skills.

The students with mental retardation should be given opportunities to exhibit the expected behaviours and responses such as everyday events listening to another person, asking questions, providing information, telling a story and expressing emotions.

School personnel should emphasis the necessity in developing the work habits and behaviours that all students will need when they begin responsible jobs.

The important work behaviours are the ability to follow instruction, cooperate with co-workers, accept supervision and maintain quality and quantity of work.

Before placing on a job, analyze the job site and study the environment. As a precaution, prepare the student to handle the hazardous situation.

Check Your Progress

- What are the important daily living skills to be taught at pre-vocational level.
- Discuss the relationship between daily living skills and vocational skills.
- How will you teach to buy and prepare food? Explain with relevant activities.
- Is it possible to teach persons with mental retardation good inter-personal skills? Specify the skills. Explain it with few activities.
- Mention the important work behaviours.

Assignment/Activities

Prepare an activity list to teach the mentally retarded persons the skills given below:

- Maintaining a home.
- Buying and preparing food.
- Preparing good quality products.
- Punctuality.

Points for Discussion/Clarification

....

....

....

....

REFERENCE

Kosako, C. (1998), *Carrer Education for the Handicapped Individuals* (2nd Edition) Lond: Charles, E. Merril.

UNIT–2

Occupational Skills Related to the Job Chosen (Inclusive of Functional Academics) Health/Safety Skills–Understanding Danger–Uses Sharp Objects, Safety Use of Household Electrical Items – First-Aid

STRUCTURE

- Introduction
- Objectives
- Work Education and Related Competencies
- Modules for Core Component of Work Education Health and Safety
- First-Aid
- Resuscitation Techniques
- Unit Summary
- Check Your Progress
- Assignment/ Activities
- Points for Discussion/Clarification
- References

2

Occupational Skills Related to the Job Chosen (Inclusive of Functional Academics) Health/Safety Skills–Understanding Danger–Uses Sharp Objects, Safety Use of Household Electrical Items–First-Aid

Introduction

During primary and secondary years, the students are given more importance to learn functional academic skills, such as reading, writing and arithmetic. This must be the primary emphasis during these years because academic skills lay the foundation for subsequent learning of the daily living and occupational skills needed for community living and working.

At pre-vocational level, a decrease in teaching academic skills should begin although much of this instruction can be decided to teaching specific daily living and occupational skills. Of course, this will vary with the mentally handicapped student and his/her potential and need for academic skills instruction. At vocational level, academic instruction should focus on subjects that the student has not yet mastered well enough and are critical to his vocational, family and community functioning.

Objectives

After learning this unit the students will be able to:

- list the competencies related to work education.
- prepare modules for the competencies and implement.
- obtain basic skills in first-aid.

Work Education Related Competencies

In Unit I, the adult living skills have been discussed in details. This unit mainly tells about the academic skills related to daily living skills. The competencies and the instructional areas related to work education are listed in the following pages:

Methods of Instruction

Select unit/competency for example, managing family finances.

List out the sub-topics/skills in this unit:

- Assess the level of the student.
- Prepare activities to teach each sub-unit.
- Give importance to practice the skills in the relevant environment—school/home/community.
- Evaluate his/her ability to practice the skills in day- to- day life.

The competencies and instructional areas worked out in this unit conserve as a work education curriculum. It is the teachers responsibility to make it suitable for each student by selecting/adding/modifying the items given in the work education programme.

Work Education

Competencies	*Instructional Area*
Managing family finances notes and making a change.	– Identifying coins, rupee – Writing cheque
Managing a home	– Decorating and maintaining class-room. – Aware of basic home repairs – Costing – Planning balanced meals – Eating proper food – Understanding the need of vitamin.
Caring for personal needs	– Physical education – Developing hygiene and grooming skills – Learning common games – Learning first-aid skills

(Contd.)

Competencies	*Instructional Area*
	– Obtaining knowledge of common illness and when to seek medical attention.
Buying and preparing food	– Mathematics – basic skills. – Developing table manners – Planning and preparing nutritious meals – Obtaining knowledge about super market – Storing food – Kitchen cleanliness.
Buying and caring for clothes	– Mathematics – English / regional language – Reading and following label directions – Using a clothes washing machine – Ironing – Selecting clothes, choosing clothes, styles and bargains,mending – Sorting clothes for laundry.
Engaging in civic activities	– Social skills – Identifying own country and state – Aware of the right for voting – Aware of personal rights as a citizen – Basic knowledge of politics – Chief-minister, governor, prime minister, president – Election.
Recreation and leisure time	– Physical education – Aware of community recreation – Spectator sports.
Getting around the community	– Reading transportation schedule – Reading traffic signs – Understanding the function of police traffic man – Planning a trip – Riding a bicycle.
Achieving self- awareness	– Identifying values and emotions – Identifying conflicts and coping with stress

(Contd.)

Competencies		*Instructional Area*
	–	Expressing feelings (anger, joy)
	–	Experiencing group interaction
	–	Developing awareness of body.
Acquiring self-confidence	–	Understanding potential of Performance
	–	Developing awareness of strength and weakness
	–	Awareness of personal behaviour
	–	Accepting praise and criticism
	–	Accepting teasing
	–	Listening actively to others.
Achieving socially responsible behaviour	–	Developing acceptable behaviour during outings
	–	Involving in activities to improve strength and overcome weakness
	–	Recognizing the rights of self and others
	–	Expressing realistic ambitions and hopes.
Maintaining adequate interpersonal skills	–	Ability to develop and maintain friendship
	–	Identifying different levels of friendship
	–	Developing self-organization in home school and community
	–	Developing ability to listen, ask questions and respond appropriately
	–	Developing appropriate relationship with opposite sex.
Achieving independence	–	Completing assigned responsibilities.
Achieving problem solving skills	–	Accepting consequences for personal action
	–	Taking assistance in difficulties.
Communicating adequately with others	–	Recognition and responding appropriately during emergency situations

(Contd.)

Competencies		*Instructional Area*
	–	Realizing the need for reading and writing.
Knowing and exploring occupational Possibilities	–	Realizing the need of work
	–	Developing an attitude to get trained and seek on employment.
Making appropriate occupational	–	Obtaining knowledge of various courses types of jobs
	–	Identifying appropriate types of work.
	–	Identifying strength and weakness for the jobs
	–	Identifying possibilities for entry level job.
Exhibiting appropriate work habits	–	Following written and verbal instructions
	–	Aware of the team concept
	–	Developing ability to take turns
	–	Developing ability to agree/disagree appropriately
	–	Developing awareness of the importance of attendance, punctuality, quality of work and productivity
	–	Realizing the need for physical exercise for well-being and success toward work and community living.

Modules for Core Component of Work Education Health and Safety

Work education activities have been categorized in two components: Core and Elective. Core group comprise of activities related to food and nutrition, safety and first-aid, environmental health, aesthetic development and enterprise education.

In this section, some modules on activities related to the core component have been included to provide guidance to teachers for conducting core activities. Keeping in view that the concept of Enterprise Education has to be integrated with the core component, some simple activities for development of entrepreneurial values and skills have been integrated with the core activities. It is expected that the teachers would try to develop some more activities such as cost calculation, buying and selling, marketing, consumers' choice, etc.

Before administering the activity, the teacher should plan the activity, ensure the availability of materials and should give clear instructions to the students. The activities should be so organized that they give opportunities to students to explore, investigate, experiment and share ideas. The activities should be followed by discussions and short stories so that the pupils may understand the concept and the message emanating from the activity and also develop positive attitude and values. The participation of all pupils should be ensured in the group activity by encouraging each child and using simple strategies to promote learning.

The activity based modular unit is divided into following sections:

1. Instructional Objectives.
2. Relevant Information.
3. Materials Required.
4. Planning and Preparation.
5. Precautions.
6. Procedure.
7. Follow up.
8. Evaluation.

Target Groups – Secondary, Pre-vocational and NIOS levels.

(i) Module 1.
(ii) Identifying Vegetables.

1. *Instructional Objectives*

Students will be able to

- identify various vegetables; and
- differentiate between different vegetables on the basis of colour, size, shape, etc.

2. *Relevant Information*

Vegetables form an important part of our daily diet. They vary in colour, shape, size, etc. Their availability also differs from season to session. They can be utilized to make pupils understand the differences in colour, shape and size, etc.

3. ***Materials Required***

- Chart of vegetables.
- Specimen of vegetables.
- Clay models of vegetables.

4. ***Planning and Preparation***

The teacher will ask the students to bring different vegetables on a particular day and should also arrange vegetable charts and clay models of vegetables.

5. ***Precautions***

- Display a vegetable chart, which shows vegetables true to the colour and shape.
- Include only fresh and healthy vegetable specimens for demonstration.

6. ***Procedure***

The teacher should:

- Display the vegetable chart at a prominent place and describe the chief characteristics of each vegetable.
- Put clay model of vegetables on different numbered places.
- Ask students to observe the displayed models and note the chief characteristics of vegetables i.e., colour, shape, etc.
- Collect all the displayed samples and put them in a basket.
- Ask students to pick vegetables one-by-one and categorize them on the basis of colour, shape, etc.
- Ask students to identify the vegetables one-by-one and count them.
- Ask why they have brought that vegetable and which vegetable they like most and why.
- Ask to visit the vegetable market along with their parents and see how their parents are buying vegetables.

7. ***Follow-Up***

The teacher should:

- ask students whether they visited the vegetable market or not.
- ask to prepare a list of vegetables purchased at home during a week.
- ask parents whether their children are identifying vegetables at home and market.

8. *Evaluation*

Place different types of vegetables and ask the students to prepare a list of vegetables. A quiz on vegetables may be organized by dividing the class into groups.

MODULE–1

Visit to Grocery Shop

1. *Instructional Objectives*

Students will be able to:

- identify different grocery items;
- read the labels of packaging of grocery items; and
- recognize identification marks for food standards.

2. *Relevant Information*

Grocery shop can be utilized to explain students about food items and its packaging details. Labels contain details about products, how to select food items, based on the descriptions given on the packing. It will also be useful in making children conscious about their duties and rights as a customer.

3. *Materials Required*

- Note-book
- Pencil/pen
- Eraser.

4. *Planning and Preparation*

The teacher should fix a date with a grocery shop owner and inform the students in advance about the visit.

5. *Precautions*

Students should be advised not to disturb items during visit and follow discipline.

6. *Procedure*

The teacher should take the students to a grocery shop and ask them to:

- prepare a list of items kept in grocery shop.
- note down the contents of the labels of the packaged foods.
- discuss about the variations in the composition of different grocery items.
- explain the parameters that should be considered while purchasing grocery items.

7. *Follow-Up*

The teachers should explain the students about the importance of quality certification by the Government agency such as AGMARK marks in selecting grocery items and ask to collect more information about the importance of certification of food items.

8. *Evaluation*

The students may occasionally be asked whether they are following the practice to buy certified food items:

MODULE–2

Sprouting of Pulses Cereals

1. *Instructional Objectives*

Students will be able to:

- understand the advantages of sprouted grains;
- select pulses and cereals for sprouting; and
- sprout pulses and cereals.

2. *Relevant Information*

The sprouted grains serve as a good source of nutrition. Children should eat sprouted gram, mung, wheat, etc. in their breakfast. The method of sprouting pulses and cereals is very simple and easy. Sprouting is done by soaking pulses and cereal grains in water, using a wet cloth. Soaking is done for a particular duration. Care has to be taken while sprouting grains, as over or under soaking is not desirable.

3. *Materials Required*

- Mung
- Gram
- Wheat
- White muslin cloth
- Potable water
- Container
- Onion
- Salt
- Lemon
- Chat Masala
- Tomato

4. *Planning and Preparation*

Teacher will collect/ask students to bring mung/gram/wheat grains and white muslin cloth.

5. *Precaution*

- Clean pulses should be used for sprouting.
- Pure water should be used.
- Clean cloth must be used for sprouting grains.

6. *Procedure*

The teacher should:

- ask students to visually inspect the grains of pulses and cereals.
- ask to wash grains and tie them in a muslin cloth.
- place the muslin cloth in a container or hang the same at a safe place.
- ask to spray water on the grains periodically (at an internal of 2-3 hrs) and observe for sprouts after 12 to 18 hours.
- transfer the sprouts to a plate, once proper sprouting has taken place, and sprinkle finely, cut pieces of onion, tomato, salt, chat masala and lemon over the sprouted pulses and cereals.
- distribute the sprouted grains to students for eating.
- ask to see sprouting/germination in different seasons.
- ask to calculate the cost of sprouted grain chat.

7. *Follow-Up*

The teacher will ask students to carry out this activity at home.

8. *Evaluation*

Students may be asked to prepare a list of items, which are used for preparing sprouted grain chaat.

MODULE–3

Washing Hands Before and After Meals

1. *Instructional Objectives*

Students will be able to:

- explain the importance of good eating habits; and
- practice good eating habits at school and home.

2. *Relevant Information*

Good eating habits are necessary for avoiding illness due to contaminated food. Good habits help in good table manner.

3. *Materials Required*

- Tiffin box.
- Water bottle.
- Napkins.

4. *Planning and Preparation*

No specific preparation is required.

5. *Precautions*

Students should wash their hands properly.

6. *Procedure*

The teacher should:

- ask students to sit in a clean and dry place.
- ask to wash their hands with soap and clean water before taking food.
- explain the bad effects of not washing hands before taking food.

- observe whether the children are taking food properly and ate food not spreading it here and there.
- ask to wash their hands and mouth.
- ask to dry hands with a clean napkin/towel.

7. *Follow-Up*

The teacher should observe whether the students are practicing healthy eating habits regularly. The teacher can write a note to the parents to observe the practice regularly at home.

8. *Evaluation*

After observation of the practice in the school, the teacher should award grades.

MODULE–4

Safety and First-Aid, Handling Electricity, Gas etc.

1. *Instructional Objectives*

Students will be able to:

- understand precautions, which should be taken while operating electrical items; and handle electrical gadgets safely.

2. *Relevant Information*

Electricity plays an important role in daily life. Without electricity it is very difficult to imagine a comfortable life. At the same time, if it is not handled properly, it can prove to be fatal.

3. *Materials Required*

- Charts of do's and don'ts related to use of electrical gadgets.
- Tester.
- Dry wood.
- Rubber slipper.
- Electrical appliances.

4. *Planning and Preparation*

The teacher should study the manual for understanding the procedures to be adopted for safe handling of electrical gadgets. The teachers should also arrange charts of do's and don'ts related to the use of electrical gadgets.

5. *Precautions*

The teacher should inform pupils about the precautions to be taken while handling the electrical gadgets.

6. *Procedure*

The teacher should:

- display all the items on a prominent place.
- describe the parts and functioning of different electrical gadgets.
- explain about the do's and don'ts related to the electrical gadgets/appliances, such as:

  (*a*) never touch bare wire.
  (*b*) never temper with any electrical item in which current is passing.
  (*c*) never disconnect a plug point by pulling wire.
  (*d*) switch off and disconnect electrical gadgets before touching or handling.
  (*e*) always handle electrical gadgets with dry hands.
  (*f*) never throw water when appliance is connected with electricity.
  (*g*) report to concerned authority in case of defective or broken wire plug, etc.
  (*h*) in case of electric shock, artificial respiration should be given, if needed.
  (*i*) check the current with tester in case there is any doubt.
  (*v*) ask pupils to enact play on the safe use of electrical gadgets.

7. *Follow-Up*

The teacher may ask students that whether they are taking precautions in using electrical gadgets. The teacher may also share his/her experiences with students.

8. *Evaluation*

The teacher may ask questions on safety measures related to the use of electrical gadgets.

First-Aid

1. *Burns*

Burns result from dry heat, extreme cold, corrosive substances, friction or radiation, including the sun's rays; scalds are caused by wet heat from hot liquids and vapours. Burns and scalds may be associated with conditions that pose a greater threat to life or there may be other serious injuries caused. Once the burns are treated, the casualty should be thoroughly examined.

Pretreatment Considerations

Before treating a burn, it is important to consider the extent and depth of the burn, its cause and whether the airway is affected.

The extent of the burn will tell you whether shock is likely to develop because of excessive loss of tissue fluid (serum). Burns destroy the skin, the body's natural barrier against airborne bacteria, and therefore carry a serious risk of infection: the deeper the burn, the higher the risk.

Once you are able to establish the cause of the burn, you can decide on the treatment. If the airway has been injured, the casualty may experience breathing difficulties, which will require urgent attention.

1. How burns are caused:

Type of burn	*Causes*
Dry burn	Flame, contact with hot objects for example domestic appliances or cigarettes, friction.
Scald	Steam, hot liquids such as tea and coffee.
Electrical burns	Low voltage current as used by domestic appliances, high voltage currents as carried in overhead cables, lightning strikes.
Cold injury	Frostbite, contact with freezing metals, contact with freezing vapours such as liquid oxygen or liquid nitrogen.
Chemical burns	Industrial chemicals, including inhaled fumes and corrosive gases, domestic chemicals and agents such as

(Contd.)

Type of burn	*Causes*
	paint stripper, caustic soda, weed killers, bleach, oven cleaner or any other strong acid or alkali.
Radiation burn	Sunburn, over-exposure to ultra violet lamp ("sunlamp"), exposure to radioactive source, such as an X-ray.

Extent of Burns

It is vital to assess the extent of the area affected by a burn, as the greater the surface area, the greater the fluid loss and risk of shock. By using a simple formula, "the rule of nines", that divides the body into area of about nine per cent, you can calculate the extent and decide what medical aid is needed.

If in doubt, call a doctor. For an adult:

- Any partial thickness burn of one per cent or more must be seen by a doctor;
- A partial thickness burn of over nine per cent will cause shock to develop and the casualty will need hospital treatment.
- Any full thickness burn requires hospital treatment. A child with any partial or full thickness burns needs medical attention.

If 60 per cent of the skin surface (40% in the very young or old) is burned, kidney failure is likely to occur up to six weeks after the burn is sustained.

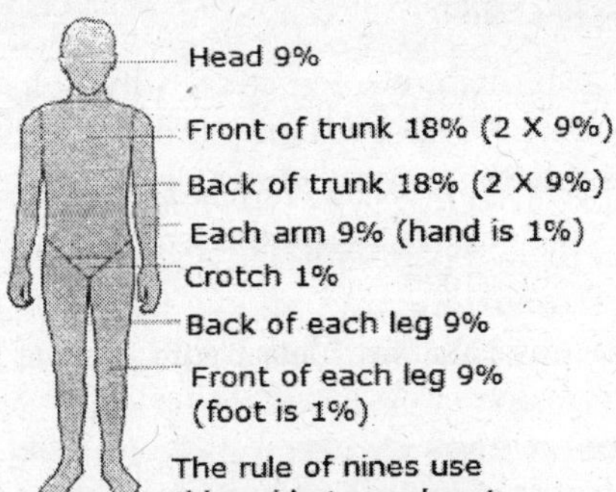

The rule of nines use this guide to work out the extent of a burn as a percentage of the body's surface area.

Depth of Burns

There are three types of burn injury: superficial, partial thickness, and full thickness. A casualty may suffer one or more depths of burn in an accident. In very deep burns, pain sensation is usually lost, which may mislead both you and the casualty about the true severity of the injury.

Superficial Burn

This involves only the outermost layer of skin and is characterized by redness, swelling and tenderness. It usually heals well if first-aid is given promptly, and should not require medical attention unless it is extensive.

Partial Thickness Burn

Any one per cent burn affecting layers of the epidermis, giving rise to rawness and blisters, needs medical treatment. Such burns can heal well, but if they affect very large area (i.e. over 60%) of the body, they can be fatal.

Full Thickness Burn

With this type of burn, all the layers of the skin are burned and there may be some damage to nerves, fat tissues, and muscles. The skin may look waxy, pale, or charred. Urgent medical attention is always essential for these burns.

Treatment of Burn

- *Minor Burns and Scalds*

Small, superficial burns are often caused by domestic accidents. Most can be treated by a First-Aider and will heal naturally. If you are in any doubt as to the severity of the injury, seek medical advice.

1. Flood the injured part with cold water for at least ten minutes to stop the burning and relieve the pain. If water is not available, any cold, harmless liquid, such as milk or canned drinks, will do.
2. Gently remove any jewellery, watches, belts, or constricting clothes from the injured area before it begins to swell.
3. Cover the area with a sterile dressing, or any clean non-fluffy material and bandage loosely in plane

■ *Blisters*

Thin "bubbles", known as blisters, form on skin that has been damaged by heat or friction. They are caused by tissue fluid (serum) leaking into the burned area below the skin's surface. During healing, new skin forms at the base of the blister; the serum is reabsorbed and the outer layer of dead skin will eventually peel off.

Treatment of Severe Burns and Scalds

Great care must be taken when treating burns that are deep or extend over a large area. The longer the burning continues, the more severe the injury will be. If the casualty has been burned in a fire, it should be assumed that smoke or hot air has also affected the respiratory system.

1. Lay the casualty down. Protect the burned area from contact with the ground, if possible.
2. Douse the burn with plenty of cold liquid. Thorough cooling may take at least ten minutes, but must not delay the casualty's removal to hospital.
3. While cooling the burn, watch for signs of difficulty in breathing, and be ready to resuscitate if necessary.
4. Gently remove any rings, watches, belts, shoes, or smouldering clothing from the injured area, before it begins to swell. Carefully remove burned clothing, unless it is sticking to the burn.
5. Cover the injury with a sterile dressing or some other suitable material to protect it from germs and infection.
6. Gather and record details of the casualty's injuries, circumstances and potential hazards such as gas.
7. While waiting for help, reassure the casualty and treat for shock. Monitor and record her breathing and pulse rates, and be prepared to resuscitate if necessary.

Special Types of Burns and Preventions

Many burns are caused not by direct contact with a naked flame, but by scorching air or heat produced within the body tissues by, for example, electricity. The damage caused in the same as that in thermal burns and first-aid follows the same principles. With accidents involving high voltage electricity or harmful chemicals, remember that your own safety comes first. Do not endanger yourself or others by treating a casualty in hazardous circumstances, however urgent the casualty's needs appear.

■ *Burns to the Airway*

Burns to the face and within the mouth and throat are very dangerous, as the air passage rapidly become inflamed and swollen. Usually, signs of burning will be evident, but you should always suspect burns to the airways if the injury has been sustained in a confined space, as the casualty may have inhaled hot air or gases.

There is no specific first-aid treatment for an extreme case; the swelling will rapidly block the airways, and there is a serious risk of suffocation. Immediate and specialized medical-aid is required. Your aims are: (1) To obtain specialist for medical-aid as quickly as possible. (2) To maintain an open airway.

■ *Electrical Burns*

Burns may occur when electricity passes through the body. Much of the visible damage occurs in the point of entry and exit of the current. However, there may also be a track of internal damage. The position and direction of entry and exit wounds will alert you to the likely extent of the hidden injury, and to the degree of shock that may ensue.

1. Make sure that contact with the electrical source is broken.
2. Flood the sites of injury with plenty of cold water to cool the burns, and cut away any burned clothing if necessary.
3. Place a sterile dressing, a clean, folded triangular bandage, or some other clean, non-fluffy material over the burns to protect them against nay airborne infection.

■ *Chemical Burns*

Certain chemicals may irritate, harm, or be absorbed through the skin, causing widespread and sometimes fatal damage. Unlike thermal burns, the signs develop slowly, but the first-aid is the same.

Most strong corrosives are found in industry, although chemical burns do occur in the home, especially from dishwasher products (the most frequent cause of alkali burns in children), oven cleaners, and paint stripper.

Chemical burns are always serious and may require urgent hospital treatment. If possible, note the name and brand name of the substance. Ensure your safety : some chemicals give off deadly fumes.

1. First make sure that the area is safe. Ventilate the area and, if possible, seal the chemical container. Remove the casualty from the area if necessary.
2. Flood the affected area with water to disperse the chemical and to stop the burning. Do this for longer than for a thermal burn – at least 20 minutes.
3. Gently remove any contaminated clothing while flooding the injury.
4. Take or send the casualty to hospital; watch the airway and breathing closely. Note and pass on any details about the chemical to medical personnel.

2. *Chemical Burns to the Eye*

Splashes of chemicals in the eye can cause serious injury if not treated quickly. Chemicals can damage the surface of the eye, resulting in scarring and even blindness. When irrigating the eye, be specially careful that the contaminated rinsing water does not splash you or the casualty. Wear protective gloves if they are available. Do not allow the casualty to touch the injured eye or forcibly remove contact lens.

1. Hold the affected eye under gently running cold water for at least ten minutes. Make sure that you irrigate both sides of the eyelid thoroughly. You may find it easier to pour the water from an irrigator or a glass. If the eye is shut in a spasm of pain, gently but firmly pull the eyelids open. Be careful that contaminated water does not splash the injured eye.
2. Ask the casualty to hold a sterile eye pad or a pad of clean, non-fluffy material over the injured eye.
3. Take or send the casualty to hospital. Identify the chemical, if possible.

Action

- *Cool Burn:* Make the casualty comfortable; pour cold liquid on the injury for ten minutes, while cooling watch signs for difficulty in breathing. Be ready to resuscitate if required.

Burns Treatment Precaution

Do Not apply lotions, ointment or fat to a burn, or touched the injured area or bursts any blisters.

Do Not remove anything sticking to the burn.

If the burn is to the face, do not cover it. Keep cooling with water until help arrives.

If the burn is large or deep, treat the casualty for shock.

Monitor and record breathing, pulse and level of response every ten minutes.

If the burn is chemical, rinse for at least 20 minutes.

- *Remove any constriction:* Carefully remove any clothing or jewellery from the affected area before the injury starts to swell.
- *Cover burn:* Cover the burn and surrounding area with a sterile dressing or a clean piece of material, reassure the casualty.
- *Take or send casualty to hospital:* Call an ambulance and send the casualty to hospital.

Burns Action and Safety

Fires

- **Do Not** attempt to fight a fire unless it is safe and you have called the emergency services.
- **Do Not** enter a burning building.
- **Do Not** enter a smoke or fume filled room.

Preventions

Call Fire Brigade; remove the casualty from danger, if it is safe to do so.

Clothing on Fire

- **Do Not** use flammable materials to try to smother flame.
- **Do Not** let the casualty run about or go outdoors.

Preventions

STOP, DROP, WRAP and ROLL the casualty on the ground; or lay the casualty down, burning side upwards and douse him with water.

Electrical Injuries

- **Do Not** go within 18 meters of live high-voltage electrical sources.
- **Do Not** touch electrical wire with wet hand.
- **Do Not** do electrical work with naked feet, always wear slipper.
- If there is a leakage in electric wiring immediately put the main off.

Preventions

Stay clear of the casualty until;

- You have switched off a domestic current; or
- You have been officially informed that a high voltage current has been switched off and isolated.

Chemical Burns

- **Do Not** delay starting treatment by searching for antidote.
- Never attempt to neutralize acid or alkali burns.

Preventions

- Protect yourself from corrosive chemicals.
- Make sure that any contaminated rinsing water drains away safely.
- Be aware of the dangers of toxic fumes.
- Seal the chemical container, if possible ventilate the area.

3. *Injuries*

Injuries are caused from accidents, which may vary from mild to severe. Accident may occur anywhere, anytime. In workshop, while working many accidents might happen, this may result in mild to severe bleeding.

While working with hacksaw blade, the palm or wrist or in general hand may cut, type of wound also varies according to the movement of the blade.

While working in lathe machine, care should be taken in the movement of hand, if accidentally the finger gets into the thread of the machine, it may get crushed. Possibly this may be amputated in future. Here we will discuss the general first-aid for all kind of injuries.

Severe External Bleeding

Massive external bleeding is dramatic and distressing, and may distract you from first-aid priorities.

Treatment

Your Aims are

- To control the bleeding.
- To prevent and minimize the effects of shock.
- To minimize the risk of infection.
- To arrange urgent removal of casualty to hospital.

1. Remove or cut clothing to expose the wound. Watch out for sharp objects, such as glass, that may injure you.
2. Apply direct pressure over the wound with your fingers or palm, preferably over a sterile dressing or clean pad, but do not waste time hunting for a dressing. If you cannot apply direct pressure, for example, if an object is protruding, press down firmly on either side.
3. Raise and support an injured limb above the level of the casualty's heart. Handle the limb very gentle if the injury involves fracture.
4. Lay the casualty down. This will reduce the blood flow to the site of the injury and minimize shock.
5. Leaving any original pad in place, apply a sterile dressing. Bandage it in place firmly, but not so tightly as to impede the circulation. If bleeding seeps through the dressing, bandage another firmly over the top. If there is a protruding foreign body, build-up padding on either side of the object until high enough to bandage over the object without pressing on it.
6. Secure and support the injured part with bandaging.
7. Treat for shock. Check the dressing for seepage. Check the circulation beyond the bandage.

Wounds at Special Sites

Scalp and Head Wounds

The scalp has a rich blood supply, and when it is damaged, the skin splits producing a gaping wound. Bleeding may be profuse and will often make the injury appear worse than it is. However, a scalp wound may be part of a more serious underlying injury, such as a skull fracture, examine the casualty very carefully, particularly if he or she is elderly, or when it is possible that a serious head injury is masked by alcohol or drug intoxication.

Treatment and Management

1. Wearing disposable gloves, if possible, replace any displaced skin flaps.
2. Apply firm direct pressure over a sterile dressing or clean pad.
3. Secure the dressing with a roller bandage. Lay the casualty down with head and shoulders slightly raised.

Take or send the casualty to hospital in the final treatment position.

Wounds to the Palm

The palm is richly supplied with blood and a wound may bleed profusely. A deep wound may severe tendons and nerves and result in loss of feeling in the fingers. If a foreign body prevents fist clenching.

Treatment and Management

1. Press a sterile dressing or clean pad firmly into the palm and ask the casualty to clench his fist over it. If he finds it difficult to press hard, he may grasp the fist with his uninjured hand.
2. Bandage the casualty's fingers so that they are clenched over the pad. Tie the knot over his fingers.
3. Support the casualty's arm in an elevation sling and arrange to take him or her to hospital.

Wound at Joint Creases

Major blood vessels cross the inside of the elbow and knee and if severed will bled copiously. Remember that the technique described below will, by compressing the artery, impede the blood supply to the lower part of the limb.

1. Press a clean pad over the injury. Blend the joint as firmly as possible.
2. With the joint firmly bent to press on the pad, raise the limb. If possible lay the casualty down to reduce the shock.
3. Take or send the casualty to hospital in the treatment position. Release the pressure briefly every ten minutes to restore normal blood flow.

Wound at Varicose Veins

1. Lay the casualty on her back and raise the injured leg as high as possible. This may reduce or stop the bleeding.
2. Expose the site of the bleeding and apply firm direct pressure over a sterile dressing or clean pad with a securing bandage or with your fingers until bleeding is controlled.
3. Remove garments such as garters or elastic topped stockings that may be impeding blood flow back to the heart.
4. Put a large, soft pad over the dressing, bandage it firmly enough to exert even pressure, but not so tightly that the circulation is impeded.
5. Keep the injured leg is raised and supported until the ambulance arrives.

Crush Injuries

These are commonly caused by traffic accidents and incidents during building work, and by train crashes, explosions, earthquakes or mining accidents.

Local injuries may include fractures, swelling, blistering and internal bleeding. The crushing force may also impair the circulation, causing numbness below the site of injury; there may be no detectable pulse in a crushed limb.

The Dangers of Prolonged Crushing

If the casualty is trapped for any length of time, two serious complications may endanger him. Firstly, prolonged crushing may cause extensive damage to tissue especially to muscles. Once the pressure is removed, shock may develop rapidly as tissue fluid leaks into the injured area.

Secondly, and more dangerously, toxic substances will build up in damaged muscle tissue around a crush injury. If released suddenly into the circulation, these toxins may cause kidney failure. This process called "crush syndrome" is extremely serious and can be fatal.

For a Casualty Crushed for Less than Ten Minutes

Release the casualty as quickly as possible.

Control any external bleeding and cover any wounds.

Secure and support any suspected fractures.

Examine and observe the casualty for signs of shock and treat accordingly.

For a Casualty More than Ten Minutes

1. Call Ambulance and give clear details of the incident first.
2. Comfort and reassure the casualty until help arrives.

Impalement

If someone becomes impaled by, for example, falling on railings, you must never attempt to raise him or her off; you may worsen internal injuries. Give clear details to the emergency services, they will bring specialist cutting equipment.

Treatment and Management

1. Explain the situation clearly and send someone to make the call, if possible.
2. Support the casualty's weight so that he or she is as comfortable as possible. Constantly reassure the casualty.

4. *Epilepsy and Other Conditions*

A convulsion, or fit, consists of involuntary contractions of many of the muscles in the body, caused by a disturbance in the function of brain. Convulsions usually result in loss of, or impaired consciousness. There are number of possible causes, including head injury, some brain damaging diseases, shortage of oxygen to the brain, and the intake of certain poisons. In babies and young children, fits may be triggered by high temperature. Fits are also the feature of epilepsy.

Convulsions – Rules of Treatment

No matter what the cause of fit, one must observe the three rules of treatment for the unconscious casualty like:

1. Ensure that the airway is clear.
2. Keep checking the response level.
3. Examine the casualty thoroughly.

Protect the casualty from further harm during a fit, and arrange appropriate after care.

Types of Epilepsy

Minor Epilepsy

Short of major epilepsy, there are many forms of epilepsy, including absence seizures which cause only a brief blurring of consciousness, like day dreaming. On recovery the casualty may simply have lost the thread of what he or she was doing. The level of consciousness varies in all forms of minor epilepsy, but a major fit sometimes follows a minor one.

Recognition

There may be

1. sudden "switching off"; the casualty may be staring blankly ahead.
2. slight or localized twitching or jerking of the lips, eyelids, head or limbs.
3. odd automatic movements such as lip smacking, chewing or making noises.

Treatment

1. Help the casualty to sit down in a quiet place. Remove any, possible sources of harm, for example hot drinks, or sharp objects from the immediate vicinity.
2. Talk to her calmly and reassuringly. Do not pester her with questions. Stay with her until you are sure she is herself again.

If the casualty does not recognize and know about her condition, advise her to consult her own doctor as soon as possible.

Major Epilepsy

This condition is characterized by recurrent, major disturbances of brain activity, resulting in violent seizures (tonic-clonic) and severe impairment of consciousness. Epileptic fits can be sudden and dramatic, but the casualty may have a brief warning period (aura) with for example a strange feeling of a special smell or taste.

Recognition

An epileptic fit usually follows a pattern:

1. The casualty suddenly falls unconscious, often letting out a cry.
2. He becomes rigid, arching his back (this is known as tonic phase).
3. Breathing may cease, the lips may show a grey-blue tinge (cyanosis) and the face and neck may become congested.
4. Convulsive movements begin (the clonic phase). The jaw may be clenched ar d breathing may be noisy. Saliva may appear at mouth, blood stained if lips and tongue have been bitten. There may be loss of bowel and bladder control.
5. The muscles relax and breathing becomes normal; the casualty recovers consciousness, usually within a few minutes. He may fell dazed or behave strangely in a state of automatism being unaware of his actions. A fit may also be followed by deep sleep.
6. There may be evidence of injury, such as burns or scars, from previous fits.

Treatment

1. If you see the casualty falling, try to support him or ease his fall. Make space around him and ask bystanders to move away.
2. Loosen clothing around his neck and if possible protect his head.
3. When the convulsions cease, place him in the recovery position. Check breathing and pulse and be prepared to resuscitate if necessary Stay with him until he is fully recovered.
4. If he is unconscious for more than ten minutes or convulsing for more than five, is having repeated fits or his first fit, or is

unaware of his conditions, don't forget to call for ambulance for emergency action.

Treatment of Convulsions in Case of Younger Children

1. Remove any clothes or covering bed-clothes. Ensure a good supply of cool, fresh air (caution – not to overcool the child).
2. Position pillows or soft padding around the child so that even violent movement will not result in injury.
3. Sponge the child with tepid water to help cooling, start at her head and work down.
4. Keep the airway open, by using the recovery position if possible.
5. Cater until the ambulance arrives.

5. *Suffocation*

Disorders of Respiration

Any disturbance of the respiratory process is potentially fatal, since it may lead to suffocation, a condition caused not only by smothering, but also by any condition that stops oxygen being taken up from the lungs by the blood.

The depletion of oxygen in the body is known as hypoxia. In this state the tissues begin to deteriorate rapidly-brain cells will start to die if their oxygen supply is interrupted for as little as three minutes.

The medical term for suffocation is asphyxia. Suffocation is often thought to result from a physical barrier to the airway, and associated with smothering.

In fact, suffocation occurs when life is threatened because the breath is deficient in oxygen. Suffocation can therefore result not just from an airway obstruction but also from contamination of the air with, for example, fumes or carbon monoxide that interfere with the ability of the blood to absorb oxygen.

General Signs and Symptoms

- Noisy, laboured breathing.
- Grey-blue skin (cyanosis).
- Flaring of the nostrils.

- Reversed movement of the chest while breathing; the chest wall will suck in as the casualty breathes in.
- Drawing in of the chest wall between the ribs and of the soft spaces above the collar bones and breastbone.

Management

Aims are

- to restore a supply of fresh air to the casualty's lungs.
- to seek medical help.

  Remove any obstruction to the casualty's breathing, such as debris restricting chest movement or anything over the mouth and nose. If needed move the casualty to the fresh air.
- if the casualty is unconscious, open the airway, check breathing and pulse and be ready to resuscitate.
- if the casualty is conscious, reassure her, but keep her under observation. Call a doctor, even if she seems to have recovered completely.

Neurological—{unconsciousness, fainting (signs, symptoms, management)}

Disorders of Consciousness

The nervous system is the most highly developed system in the body; it controls consciousness, contains centers for memory, speech, thought and will and correlates the activities of other body systems.

A fully conscious person is awake, alert and aware of his surroundings. Sleep is a normal state of lowered consciousness, but unconsciousness is an abnormal state in which the body's control mechanisms are impaired or lost. When a person is asleep, vital functions such as breathing take place automatically. If a person is unconscious, muscle control is lost, so if the person is lying on his or her back, the tongue falls towards the back of the throat and may block the airway. An unconscious casualty will therefore require immediate first aid.

Unconsciousness and Impaired Consciousness

There are number of disorders that cause varying levels of impaired or lost consciousness; after checking the airway, breathing and pulse you must establish the level of (un) consciousness.

First -Aid Priorities

- Open an unconscious casualty's airways. Every few minutes, check the airway, breathing and circulation. Record the breathing and pulse rates.
- Protect the casualty from harm.
- Monitor and record the level of response.
- Look for and treat for associated injuries.
- If unconsciousness lasts for more than three minutes or if you suspect a serious condition such as stroke or skull fracture, arrange urgent removal of the casualty to hospital.

Whatever, the cause for unconsciousness follow three rules:

- *Ensure that airway is clear:* An unconscious casualty's airway is in constant danger, particularly if he or she is lying face up. The tongue may flop to the back of the throat and the muscles that normally keep the airway open and the cough reflex that clears saliva from the throat will not function. Stomach contents may be rerurgitated and inhaled.

- *Keep checking the response level:* There are many degrees of impaired awareness and response short of full unconsciousness (coma). Make a rapid assessment using the "AVPU" code. Make a detailed assessment using a simplified version of the Glasgow Coma Scale. Repeat every ten minutes.

- *Examine the casualty thoroughly:* Impaired consciousness can mask other injuries, so a full examination is vital. The casualty's condition and level of response may alter with timo. To avoid aggravating any spinal injuries do not move the casualty unnecessarily.

Eyes – do they:	*Movement – does the casualty*	*Speech – does the casualty*
Open spontaneously? Open on command? Open to a painful stimulus?	Obey commands? Move in response to painful stimulus?	Respond sensibly to questions? Questions? Appear confused?
Remain closed?	Make no response.	Make incomprehensible sounds? Make no response?

Treatment

Your Aims are

- to lower the casualty's body temperature as quickly as possible.
- to arrange removal of the casualty to hospital.
- quickly remove the casualty to a cool place. Remove as much of his outer clothing as possible.

Wrap the casualty in a cold, wet sheet and keep it wet until his temperature falls to 38° C/100.4° F (under the tongue) or 37.5° C/.

6. *Resuscitation, Moving, Placing and Calling for Expert Attention*

For life to continue, the body requires an adequate supply of oxygen to enter the lungs and be transferred to all cells in the body through the blood stream. In particular, if the brain, the organ that controls all the bodily functions, does not have constant supply of oxygen it will begin to fail after three to four minutes. Without oxygen, the casualty will loose consciousness, the heartbeat and breathing will cease and death will result.

The ABC of Life

Three elements are involved in getting oxygen to the brain. The air passage or Airway must be open so that oxygen can enter the body. Breathing must take place so that oxygen can enter the blood stream via the lungs, and the blood must travel around the body (the circulation), taking the oxygen to all the tissues and organs, including the brain.

7. *Resuscitation*

The priority in treating any casualty is to establish and maintain effective breathing and circulation. The sequence of techniques used to sustain life in the absence of spontaneous breathing and heartbeat is known as Cardio-Pulmonary Resuscitation (CPR).

Principles of Resuscitation

For life to be sustained, a constant supply of oxygen must be maintained and delivered to the brain. The pump that maintains this circulation is called heart. If heart stops (cardiac arrest), urgent action must be taken to prevent death.

In certain cases, the use of "defibrillator" which is carried in most ambulances, can start the heart beat again, so immediate medical attention required for cardiac arrest.

The Casualty is most likely to survive if

- the flow of oxygenated blood is rapidly restored to the brain by means of artificial ventilation and chest compression Cardio-Pulmonary Resuscitation or (CPR).
- the defibrillator is used promptly.
- the casualty quickly reaches hospital to receive specialized treatment and care.

Although CPR is unlikely to restart a stopped heart, it is essential to carry it out. If it is applied correctly it will keep the circulation going and ensure that the blood supply to the brain is maintained until expert help arrives.

Cardiac Arrest – The Chain of Survival

The casualty's chances of survival are greatest when all the following steps are taken.

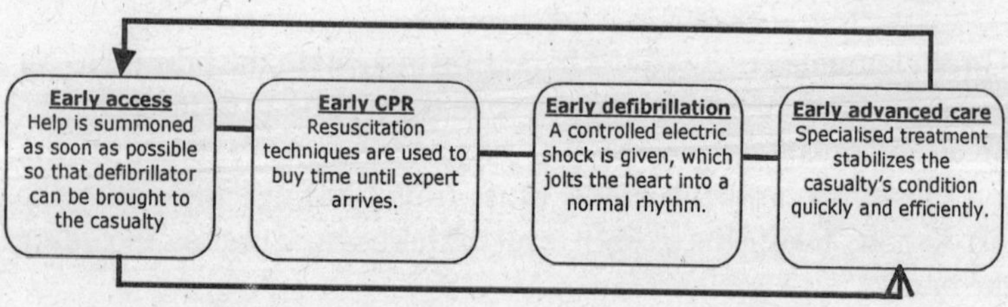

The ABC of Resuscitation:

A is for Airway	*B is for Breathing*	*C is for Circulation*
Tilting the casualty's Head back and lifting the Chin will open the airway. The tilted position lifts the Casualty's tongue from the Back of the throat so that it Does not block the air passage.	If a casualty is not breathing you can breathe for him, and thus oxygenate the blood, by giving the artificial ventilation blowing your own exhaled air in to in to the casualty's lungs.	If the heart stops, you can apply chest compression to force blood through the heart and around the body, you must combine these with Passage artificial ventilation so that the blood is oxygenated.

Resuscitation Techniques

Following techniques are used while assessing or treating the casualty who has collapsed:

The Resuscitation Sequence: (1) Check Response, (2) Open airway and check breathing, (3) Breathe for the casualty, (4) Assess for circulation and (5) Commence CPR.

1. *Check Response*

On discovering a collapsed casualty, first establish whether he or she is conscious or unconscious. Ask a sample questions such as "What has happened?" or give a command such as "Open your eyes." Speak loudly and clearly close to the casualty's ear.

If the casualty does not respond, try gently shaking his or shoulders.

- A fully unconscious casualty will make no response at all.
- The casualty may respond to pain, try gently pinching the skin.
- A casualty who is only partially conscious may mumble, groan or make slight movements.

There are different degrees of impaired awareness. One should quickly assess the casualty by using the AVPU code:

A → Alert.
V → Responds to voice.
P → Responds to pain.
U → Unresponsive.

Check Points

Eyes → do they remain closed?
Speech → does the casualty respond to the questions asked?
Movement → does the casualty obey commands? Does he respond to painful stimulus, such as pinching?

2. *Open Airway and Check Breathing*

An unconscious casualty's airway may become narrowed or blocked. This makes breathing difficult and noisy or completely impossible.

The main reason for this is that muscular control in the throat is lost, which allows the tongue to fall back and block the airway. Lifting the chin and tilting the head back lifts the tongue away from the entrance to the air passage, allowing the casualty to breathe.

To Open the Airway

Placing two fingers under the point of the casualty's chin lift the jaw. At the same time place the other hand on the casualty's forehead, and gently tilt the head well back. If any head or neck injury is there the handle the casualty carefully to avoid the casualty from further injury. Tilt the head back very slightly—just far enough to open the casualty's airway.

Checking Breathing

Kneel beside the casualty, and put your face close to his mouth. Look, listen and feel for breathing.

- Look along the chest to see if the chest rises, indicating breathing.
- Listen for sounds of breathing.
- Feel for breathe on your cheek.

Do these checks for upto ten seconds before deciding that breathing is absent.

The Recovery Position

An unconscious casualty who is breathing should be placed in recovery position. This position prevents the tongue from blocking the throat, and because the head is lower than the rest of the body, liquids can drain from the mouth, reducing the risk of the casualty inhaling stomach contents.

The head, neck and back are kept aligned, while the bent limbs keep the body propped in a comfortable and secure position. If you are forced to leave an unconscious casualty unattended, he or she can be left in recovery position while you get help.

Method of Turning the Casualty

1. Kneel beside the casualty, open his or her airway by tilting the head and lifting the chin. Straighten his or her legs. Tuck the hand nearest to you, arm straight and palm upwards,

under his or her upper thigh. Before turning him or her, remove any fragile or bulky objects from his pockets.

2. Bring the arm furthest from you across the chest, and hold the back of the hand, against the casualty's nearer cheek. With your other hand, pull up the far leg just above the knee, keeping the foot flat on the ground.
3. Keeping the casualty's hand pressed against his cheek, pull on the upper leg to roll the casualty towards you and on to his side.
4. Use your knees to support the casualty so that he is prevented from rolling too far forwards.
5. Tilt the head back to ensure the airway remains open. If necessary, adjust the hand under the cheek.
6. Adjust the upper leg, if necessary, so that both the hip and the knees are bent at right angles.
7. Adjust the lower arm so that the casualty is not lying on it. Make sure that his hand is still positioned with the palm facing upwards.

3. *Breathe for the Casualty*

The body especially the brain requires oxygen to keep the cell alive. The air that you breathe out still contains 16 per cent oxygen, so it can save life if it is blown into the casualty's lungs (artificial ventilation). If the pulse is absent, artificial ventilation must be combined with chest compression (cardiopulmonary resuscitation CPR), otherwise the oxygen will not reach the vital organs of the body.

Giving Mouth-to-Mouth Ventilation

(*a*) With the casualty lying flat on his back, remove any obvious obstruction including broken or displaced dentures from the mouth. Leave well lifting dentures in place.

(*b*) Open the airway by tilting the head and using two fingers to lift the chin.

(*c*) Close the casualty's nose by pinching it with your index finger and thumb. Take a full breathe, and place your lips around his mouth, making a good seal.

(*d*) Blow in to the casualty's mouth until you see the chest rise. Take about two seconds for full inflation.

(*e*) Remove your lips and allow the chest to fall fully, which takes about four seconds. Repeat these once and then assess for signs of circulation.

Note

1. If the pulse is absent and there are no signs of recovery, such as return of skin colour or any movement, such as swallowing, coughing or breathing, begin cardiopulmonary resuscitation immediately.
2. If the pulse is present, continue ventilations and check the pulse after every ten breathes.
3. If breathing returns, place the casualty in the recovery position.

If the Chest does not Rise

If after attempting two artificial ventilations the chest does not rise, check that:

1. the head is tilted sufficiently far back;
2. you have closed the nostrils completely;
3. you have a firm seal around the casualty's mouth;
4. the airway is not obviously obstructed by vomit, blood or a foreign body.

Clearing an Obstruction

1. If you can see any obvious obstruction inside the mouth, use your finger to hook it out carefully.
2. Attempt three further breathes. If after carrying out the above checks again, the chest still does not rise, treat as for checking and unconscious adults.

4. *Assess for Circulation*

Check the pulse for upto ten seconds, during which look for other signs of recovery, such as return of colour to the skin, any movement such as breathing, swallowing and coughing. If you cannot find the pulse or there are no other signs of circulation, begin chest compression immediately.

5. *Commence (CPR)*

Cardio-Pulmonary Resuscitation (CPR), If there is no pulse, this means that heart has stopped beating and you will have to provide an artificial circulation by means of chest compression. To be of any use, chest compressions must always combined with artificial ventilation. This process is known as cardio-pulmonary resuscitation or CPR in short.

Calling an Ambulance

- If you have a helper, send him or her to call an ambulance.
- If you are alone and the condition is due to injury or drowning, continue with the resuscitation sequence for one minute then call an ambulance.

Giving Chest Compressions

1. Kneel beside the casualty. Locate one of its lowermost ribs with the index and middle fingers of your hand. Slide your fingers along the rib to the point where the lowermost ribs meet at the breast-bone. Place your middle finger at this point and your index finger above it on the lower breast-bone.
2. Place the heel of your other hand on the breast-bone, and slide it down until it reaches your index finger. This is the point at which you should apply pressure.
3. Place the heel of your first hand on top of the other hand and interlock your fingers.
4. Leaning well over the casualty with your arms straight, press vertically down and depress the breast bone approximately 4-5 cm (1 ½ –2 in). Release the pressure without removing your hands.
5. Compress the chest 15 times aiming for a rate of about 100 compressions per minute. Then give two breathes of artificial ventilation. Continue this cycle of alternating 15 chest compressions with two breathes of artificial ventilation until help arrives.

Unit Summary

At prevocational level, a decrease in teaching academic skills should being although much of this instruction can be decided to teaching specific daily living and occupational skills. Of course, this will vary with the mentally handicapped student and his/her potential and need for academic skills instruction. At vocational level, academic instruction should focus on subjects that the student has not yet mastered well enough and are critical to his vocational, family and community functioning.

The teachers should have the basic knowledge on first aid so that they can teach the students in a stimulated situation.

Check Your Progress

Explain the important competencies needed at pre-vocational level to prepare the students for work.

How would you teach safety skills in a stimulated situation?

Assignment/Activities

Prepare models for the following:

- Understanding danger using sharp objects.
- Safety skills.

Points for Discussion/Clarification

....

....

....

....

REFERENCES

1. *Guidelines for Implementation of Programme in Schools* (2003). PSS Central Institute of Vocational Education (NCERT).
2. Andrews, I. (1997). *The A-Z of first-aid What to do in an emergency.* Mumbai: Blitz.
3. Fraser, W.I., Mac Gillivray, R.C. and Green, A.M. (1991). *Halla's Caring for People with Mental Handicaps.* Oxford: Butter worth Heinmann.
4. Gupta, L.C. (1995). *First-aid.* Jaypee Brothers Medical Publications Pvt. Ltd., New Delhi.
5. Maheshwari, M.C., *All you Want to Know About EPILEPSY*, The National Book Trust, India, 1998.
6. *Manual for Training of PHC Medical Officers* by Rehabilitation Council of India, 1999.
7. Michael Webb, Roy Scott, *Sir Peter Beale, First-Aid Manual,* 7th Edition, Dorling Kindersley.
8. Shanley, E. (1986). *Mental Handicap: A Hand Book of Care.* Edinburgh: Churchill Livingstone.

UNIT–3

Vocational Habilitation of Persons with Mental Retardation Pre-Vocational Training and Types of Employment Opportunities with Reference to Persons with Mental Retardation

STRUCTURE

- Introduction
- Objectives
- Definitions
- Stages of Vocational Rehabilitation/Transition from School to Work
- Planning for Transition
- Training Schedule – Transition Plan
- Curriculum
- Job Survey
- Individualizing the Transition Process
- Vocational Assessment
- The Individualized Vocational Curriculum – Job Analysis
- Vocational Training
- Types of Employment
- Unit Summary
- Check Your Progress
- Assignment/Activities
- Points for Discussion/Clarification
- References

3

Vocational Habilitation of Persons with Mental Retardation Pre-Vocational Training and Types of Employment Opportunities with Reference to Persons with Mental Retardation

Introduction

The major goal of educational system is to prepare the students to have independent living skills. The common misconception is that the preparation for employment starts immediately after schooling. To be functionally competent within a community, it is essential for an individual to show a wide array of skills. So the school curriculum should include prevocational and vocational skills at the school level itself. Students with mental handicap should get opportunity to engage themselves in different types of activities in which they express interest and have relatively some ability. The selected activities for training are likely to have generic value to several jobs in future and exposure to the activities as part of initiation into work. Work related skills would prepare the students to enter into full- fledged vocational/work area.

Objectives

After going through then unit the trainees will be able to

- define the terms related to vocational rehabilitation.
- analyze the stages of Vocational Rehabilitation/transition from school to work.
- prepare a vocational curriculum for transition.
- assess the students.
- select suitable jobs and give systematic training.

- describe various types of employment for persons with mental retardation.

Definitions

Habilitation

Habilitation is the process through which the persons born with certain impairment are helped to chanelize their residual capacities to their maximum development so that he/she could live as normal a life as possible.

Rehabilitation

Rehabilitation is "the combined and coordinated use of medical, social, educational and vocational measures for training/retraining the individual to the highest possible level of functioning ability."

Rehabilitation is the restoration of the handicapped to the fullest physical, mental, social, vocational and the economic usefulness of which he is capable. This definition is broadly accepted by various professionals working in the field of disability.

Vocational Rehabilitation

Vocational Rehabilitation means that part of the continuous and coordinated process of rehabilitation, which involves the guidance, vocational training and selective placement designed to enable a disabled person to secure and retain suitable employment.

Stages of Vocational Rehabilitation/Transition from School to Work

The parents of young adults at the transitional stage turn to their local community for vocational training and job placement assistance. The parents respond to the situation differently. Majority of them are comfortable if their children are permitted to continue in the special schools by engaging them time-pass activities. While few of them join sheltered employment, very few gets community employment placements. The vast majority of persons with mental retardation are unemployed or under-employed.

There is a great need to initiate the practice of developing and implementing an individual transition plan for students with mental retardation including all areas of support activities. This chapter explains the need, the process, and outcome of a well-planned transition plan for students with mental retardation.

Defining School to Work Transition

Transition is a carefully planned process from school to work, which should be developed and implemented for students with disabilities who have only three to five years remaining in school. An individual transition plan should be initiated by school personnel or adult service providers and involve special and vocational educators, vocational rehabilitation counsellors, parents, the students and adult service systems representative and possibly an employer (Wehman *et al.*).

The purpose of transition is to arrange for the opportunities and services that will support successful adult living, avoid institutionalization and prevent interruption of needed services.

Key Elements of Transition

- The key elements cf transition inherent in the definition are, Longitudinal vocational training throughout the primary, secondary and pre-vocational levels of schooling.
- Transition planning with the cooperation of parents and community.
- Parent, consumer and employer involvement in the transition planning process.
- Professional and community awareness and support of employment options.

Steps/Stages in Transition

Transition may be viewed as a four-step process.

1. Systematic school instruction.
2. Planning for transition
3. Placement in meaningful employment.
4. Follow-up services.

The Figure 1 explains the 4 stages of transition.

1. Systematic School Instruction

Traditionally, the vocational education has been provided to the adults and adolescent students as post school programmes. The

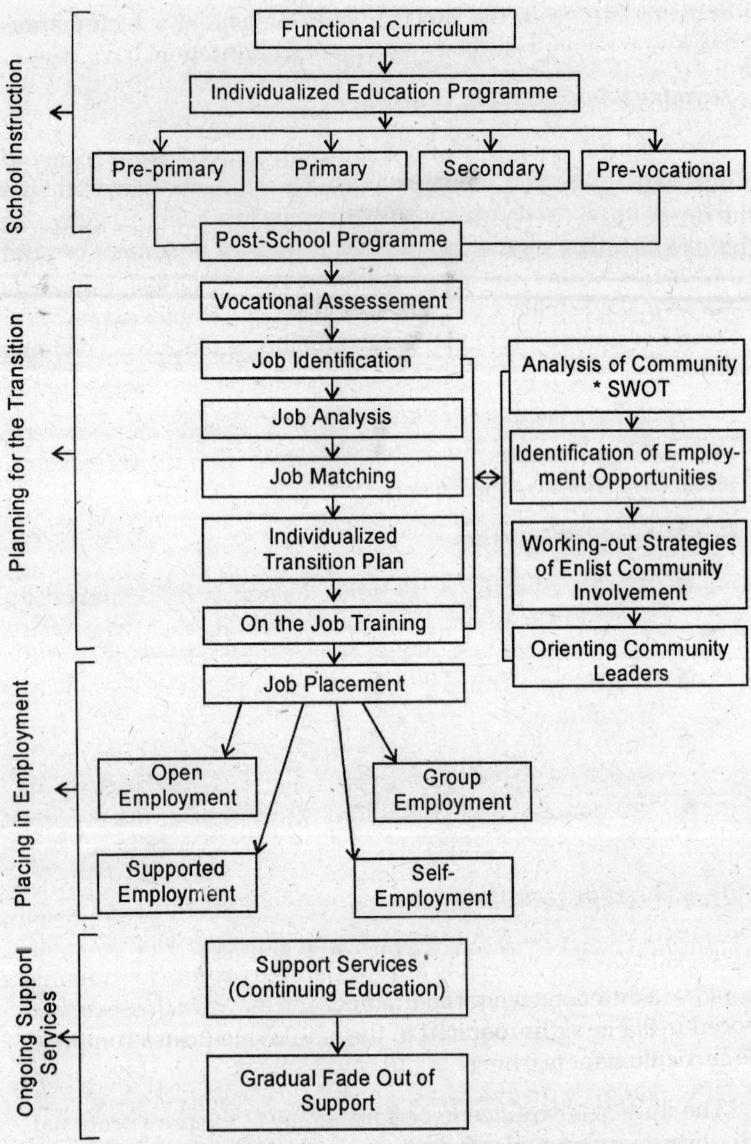

Figure 1 : Stages of Vocational Rehabilitation (NIMH Vocational Transition Model for Persons with Mental Retardation).

*SWOT – Strength, Weakness, Opportunity, Threat.

pre-vocational curriculum has been designed to provide work related skills and work skills to the age group of 14 years and above. Many a time, at the pre-vocational level, students are taught the jobs available in the sheltered workshops only.

But the recent trend is to train the mentally handicapped students in the skills that are directly useful for daily living. From the pre-primary level, the child needs to be trained in those skills that are required frequently in school, domestic, vocational and community environments. Hence, there is a need not to compartmentalize the educational and vocational activities on the logic that the pre-vocational skills are the domain of pre-vocational classes only. The pre-vocational and vocational skill training can go together with teaching of other skills to achieve the objective of making them ready to enter into work environment initially as a trainee, an apprentice and consequently as a worker.

Objectives Pre-vocational Training

- It develops work habits, positive attitudes, value toward work and daily living activities.
- It provides instructions and guidance for establishing and maintaining positive human relationships at home, school and at work.
- It develops the work skills among the students to be readily integrated physically, socially and economically into the community.

Curriculum Planning

The pre-vocational education includes the skills ranging from basic self-care survival to fairly complex work related inter-personal skills of acceptable degree. Selecting appropriate curriculum for training should be a direct outcome of community and individual assessment procedures. The skills required in the employment sites comprise the curriculum for teaching.

The student is expected to perform many of the pre-vocational activities along with his daily living activities. In all functional activities, the interaction of the non-handicapped and handicapped people is very much necessary. Now we will discuss the brushing activity and other associated pre-vocational activities that take place along with it in a rural scene.

- Collecting sticks for brushing including cutting them into correct sizes.
- Going to the appropriate brushing place – may be river or village well.
- Interacting with other non-handicapped people while brushing.
- Maintaining appropriate time for brushing.

Even in an urban setting, many prevocational activities are associated with the brushing activity. If we examine each activity, which is associated with brushing, most of them get generalized into work skills during job placement. For example: maintaining brushing time helps the student to learn maintaining the punctuality at the job site. Selection and purchasing of brush and paste help him to learn functional academics. This kind of activities strengthens the vocational skills of the student.

The term "Pre-vocational' is taken in a different perspective by most professionals. Quite often, training in prevocational activities is taken up at the prevocational level only. But prevocational activities can be taught right from pre-primary level itself, as discussed earlier. The curriculum for all levels includes self-help, motor, language, social, academics and recreational activities, but activities for work readiness skills are given more importance at prevocational level.

The goal of vocational programming at younger age is to provide student with a variety of work-experience across job types. The sampling of job types provides trainer with information regarding student's preference, differential skills, potential for progress and these are relevant to future selection of a placement site. So by the end of the prevocational level, before "on the job training', the student is likely to be competent in the necessary prerequisites of a particular job, or the student even if in the prevocational level can do part time "on the job training' in the community, if it suits him.

Developing the School Based Vocational Curriculum

Baine's Ecology Based Curriculum (Ecological Inventory) helps to develop a school based vocational curriculum. An ecological inventory can be made by listing out all functional tasks performed by the non-handicapped persons in a particular environment.

Steps to Construct the Curriculum

- Identify the target group for whom the curriculum is being designed.
- Select the target group functioning in the environment and sub environment including the boundaries of the home, community, vocational & school environment, and also predict the boundaries of the future environments.
- Identify the functional tasks that are performed by non-handicapped and handicapped individuals through interviews, observations or by giving specially designed diary to parents.
- Develop an inventory for particular handicapped individuals describing the special equipments, materials, conditions, or adaptations and methods if necessary.

Points to Consider

- The activities and the tasks, in the vocational curriculum includes are not only to be taught in the classroom but also outside the classroom, that is, in the community also. The activities, which are to be taught outside the classroom can be taken up by the teacher, parents, siblings and non-disabled persons.
- The role of non-disabled persons is to teach and assist the disabled persons while performing the functional task. The role of the handicapped persons should be encouraged to assist the non-handicapped persons while performing the same functional task.

School Based Vocational Skills training

- Make the list of the daily activities an individual performs in a particular environment.
- Identify the prevocational and vocational activities associated with the selected daily living skills.
- Prepare the Individualized Training Programme for the student including the prevocational and vocational skills along with self- help, motor, language, social, academics and recreational skills.
- Select the activities based on the age and ability level of the student.

- Encourage the parents, siblings, and other peer non-handicapped persons to participate in training.
- Train in simulated and natural settings.

The School Based Vocational Curriculum helps the students towards independent living and employability, which are the ultimate aims of special education.

Daily Living Activities	*Work Readiness Skills/ Pre-vocational Skills Associated with Daily Living Activities*
Getting up in the Morning	■ Maintaining appropriate time. ■ Folding bed. ■ Switching off lights. ■ Seeing calendar. ■ Reads the daily routine schedule. ■ Opening doors and gate.
Toileting, Bathing & Grooming	■ Reading the word TOILET. ■ Identifying the toilets for GENTS & LADIES. ■ Maintaining timings for toileting. ■ Reading the names of articles – soap, oil, shampoo, towel, bucket, mug etc., ■ Washing, drying, folding clothes. ■ Selecting appropriate dress. ■ Ironing clothes, polishing shoes, using decorants. ■ Purchasing various items from shop.
Break Fast Time	■ Helping to prepare breakfast. ■ Reading the name and prices of the items. ■ Using cooking gas or wood. ■ Measuring appropriate quantity. ■ Buying necessary items. ■ Serving breakfast. ■ Prepares lunch packet.

Training at Primary and Secondary Level

During the elementary years students with severe disabilities should be exposed to a variety of vocationally related experiences that concentrate on the development of self-care skills, social, and communication skills, awareness of vocational training opportunities and specific skill clusters that are necessary to work in a variety of potential job settings.

Training at Pre-vocational Level

During this stage, students should be provided vocational training during a large portion of the day. They should be given opportunity to practice specific job skills in a variety of job settings. These experiences should include the opportunity to acquire a variety of independent living, social, language, functional academics and community mobility skills. Money and time management, independent travel around the community, social interactions, and the ability to follow instructions and ask for help are skills that are associated with holding a job.

It is important that specific job training based on potential jobs in the student's locality be targeted during pre-vocational stage. Teaching a variety of specific work related skills in a variety of settings helps insure generalization to other work settings during job placement.

By the time a student with mental retardation is 16 years old, a minimum of three hours of the school day should be devoted to vocational training and related vocational skills. Through the development of a formal and individualized transition process, the parents, the students, and school should discuss and target a job placement with support services and training requirement.

Guidelines for Vocational Training at School Level

- Make sure the IEP addresses specific vocational training in a variety of potential jobs related to realistic employment options.
- Continue to train communication, self-care, mobility, independent living, and recreational skills. Teach all of them within the context of job training whenever possible.
- Provide job training in real job sites such as canteen, hotel, and local business centres.
- Train in a variety of school sites such as the grounds, canteen, office and overall building.
- Identify a "vocational tract" for each student so that more specific job training can occur at pre-vocational level.
- Develop a transition team and formulate a transition plan.

- Follow-up on all students who left the school to make sure they are either employed or/are receiving job placement services.

Parent Training and Involvement

An essential element to a smooth transition into work for a person with severe disabilities is the involvement of the parents/guardians. They often need training in order to understand what can be expected of their son/daughter and of which agencies can be a help on the transition team.

A major area to be included in training needs a discussion on the capabilities of individuals with severe disabilities. Because professionals and family members often tell parents that their child will never be able to develop skills for independent living, particularly competitive work, parents often have low expectations for their children. Therefore, they need to be made aware of how persons with severe disabilities can be productive on a job through a supported-work model involving a proper job match, the use of systematic instruction, the development of adaptations, and ongoing follow-up services.

Convincing parents that their children with severe disabilities will be able to work, is often difficult. Therefore, teachers and other professionals who work with elementary-age students need to be educated in the work prognosis of persons with severe disabilities. In this manner, the parent's early contact with professionals will provide more positive projections in independence.

Planning for Transition

A Case Study

It is appropriate to share the true story of Venkat, which helped him for a gradual transition from Special School to work as a helper in NIMH Library.

Venkat Narasimha is not able to talk. This is the major problem, which he faces. But he can make others understand his needs. Venkat was sent to the normal school when he was 5 years of age. Within two months, he was removed from the school due to the problem in communication and comprehension due to mild mental retardation.

Again his parents tried to get him admitted, but could not succeed. His parents, though they had to work hard to bring up their children, they wanted their son to be educated. They sought admission for Venkat at Andhra Mahila Sabha Special School at the age of 8 years. Venkat continued special education for 6 years. At the age of 14 years, he was admitted at the Special Education Centre, NIMH.

Now Let us Listen to Venkat

"I liked NIMH. I was very active and regular. I always remember my teacher. As I reached 17 years of age, the Principal was about to terminate me from the school. I was lucky to be selected to undergo training under the project 'Transition of persons with mental retardation from school to work'. I was placed at NIMH library for on-the-job training. During the initial stage, I was given a stipend of Rs. 25 per day."

I got excited when I received the first cheque and opened an account at Punjab National Bank, Manovikasnagar. I was delighted to sign, count the working days and calculate my monthly stipend. After one year training, my stipend increased upto Rs. 1,500. Currently I have an amount of Rs. 10,000 in the bank. My parents are very proud of me. Do you want to know what I do in the library as a helper?

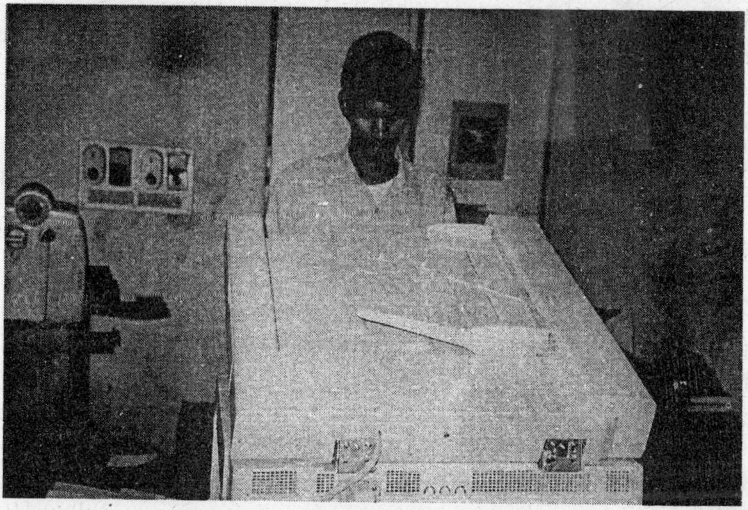

Figure 2

- Assisting in arranging books.
- Transferring books and other items.
- Distributing papers and books.
- Getting tea for staff.
- Entering book numbers and collecting tokens while distributing books.
- Photocopying.
- Setting papers for printing.

If you don't believe me, please come and see me at NIMH library as long as I am there.

I am good in floor hockey, I went to Chandigarh and Pondicherry with the team and won prizes.

The curriculum for vocational education prepared for transition from school to work is given in the following pages.

Curriculum for Vocational Education—Library Helper

Job Title: Library Helper.

Job Description

Library maintenance includes cleaning, rubbing, dusting and arrangement of furniture and books, storing and transfer of items. A fairly large library needs people to assist in their duties. A person with mental retardation is able to help in some of these duties in a library if he is trained and placed under supervision with necessary reinforcement.

Duties of a Library Helper

- Setting furniture and cleaning book shelves.
- Packing and transferring materials.
- Photocopying.

As per the nature of library and level of the trainee, more tasks can be selected.

Admission Criteria

Age: 16 years and above.

Pre-Requisite Skills

Tasks	*Prerequisite Skills*
1. Cleaning and setting	– Eye hand coordination – Sense of cleanliness – Proper vision
2. Packing and transferring	– Following instruction – Manual dexerity – Physical strength – Aware of safety
3. Photocopying and making sets of copies	– Functional Academics Second grade level – Safety handling of equipments.

Entry Level

The functional assessment checklist is used at pre-vocational level for IEP planning and implementation. For training as library helper, check on the pre-requisite skills for initiating training.

Observation

After placing 1 month in a library, observe the behaviour of the trainee and assess the work readiness skilis.

Teacher Trainee Ratio

Two trainees can be trained at a time in a library. Based on the job opportunities, select the trainee and give 1:1 training under the supervision of a staff in the library.

Duration

Duration is flexible from six months to one year based on the need of the library and the ability of the trainee.

The persons with mild mental retardation will be able to perform the above-mentioned duties. The duration is flexible. Add more tasks as he masters the above

Mode of Training

Task related academics and part 2 of the course content is taught in the classroom, job site and the community.

Training Schedule – Transition Plan

Time Schedule–Transition Plan for Vocational Education Library Helper

Duration	*Percentage of time in pre-vocational classroom*	*Skills to be taught in the class and community*	*Percentage of time at work site (Library)*	*Skills to be taught at work place*	*Evaluation and information*
Ist quarter	75% time	Basic academics	25%	Cleaning & setting	■ Assess on the checklist ■ Decide the staff respon-sible ■ Involve parents.
IInd quarter	50% time	Task related academics	50%	Packing & transferring safety skills	■ Continue assessment. ■ Send the ■ evaluation report to parents and Principal of school.
IIIrd quarter	25% time	Sex education Self advocacy	75%	Photo-copying	■ Continue assessment.
IVth quarter	–	Employability	100%	Making sets of copies	■ Final evaluation ■ Decision on placement ■ Decide whe-ther training is to be extended.

The main tasks of the job are taught in the real work setting–in library.

Curriculum

The course content is prepared in II parts. Part I is essential to work in a Library. Part II helps towards independent living.

Reinforcement

Token economy and stipend system would motivate the trainee. To teach money transaction and banking, the stipend system is necessary.

Evaluation

Periodical Evaluation

Use the checklist for Library Helper every month or at 3 months interval.

Final Evaluation

At the end of the training, prepare final evaluation report, which gives information on overall performance of the trainee.

Examination

Internal

Use the vocational education, curriculum Part 1 and Part 2 which is specially prepared for training and evaluation. 75 per cent marks for the tasks on the checklist will be given by the internal examiner for final examination.

External

25 per cent marks for the tasks on the checklist will be given by the external examiner by asking the trainee to demonstrate the tasks.

Certification

Score in each area should be mentioned and counted while preparing certificates (see the evaluation sheet). This would help the parents, placement officer and the employer to take decision on the type of tasks/assignments, which can be given to a particular trainee/employee.

This would help to continue his/her training in specific areas in which the trainee needs further training and exposure.

Placement

Based on the performance level placement decision is made.

COURSE CONTENT

Library Helper

Part – I

I. *Main Tasks Areas*

1. Setting furniture
2. Cleaning book shelves
3. Packing
4. Transferring materials
5. Photocopying

II. *Tasks Related Academics*

1. Reading symbols and numbers
2. Work schedule

III. *Safety Precautions*

1. Occupational safety
2. Symptoms of illness and medication

Part – II

1. *Basic Academics*

   1. Self and family
   2. Job site information
   3. Money transaction and banking
   4. Signals and symbols

2. *Work Place Behaviour*

   1. Etiquette and manners
   2. Personal interaction
   3. Regularity and punctuality
   4. Communication/Social behaviour
   5. Quality and quantity of work

3. *Employability*

   1. Self-awareness
   2. Job exploration
   3. Bio-data preparation
   4. Developing self-confidence
   5. Staying on job

4. *Sex Education*

   1. Anatomy and physiology
   2. Maturation or body changes
   3. Psycho social sexual behaviour
   4. Same sex behaviour
   5. Opposite sex behaviour
   6. Marriage and parenthood
   7. Leisure time and recreational activities.

5. *Self Advocacy*

   1. Basic rights
   2. Rights of living
   3. Decision-making
   4. Organizing self-advocacy groups

(For Part 2. refer curriculum for vocational Education – Transition from school to work, series 1, 2 and 3, NIMH-Publication).

Part–I

I. MAIN TASK AREAS

I. Setting Furniture *Dates:*____________

A. *Dusting and Wiping*

1. Collects all materials needed for cleaning ____________
2. Dusts the Furniture ____________
3. Wipes the furniture with cloth ____________

B. *Arrangement*

1. Aware of the place where the furniture are kept ____________
2. See that all are in proper place ____________
3. Lifts the furniture without making noice ____________
4. Does not pull the items on the floor ____________

TOTAL: ____________

2. Cleaning Book Shelves

A. *Dusting*

1. Removes and keeps the books without disturbing the order ____________
2. Dusts the book shelves ____________
3. Dusts the books ____________
4. Keeps them back carefully without disturbing order ____________
5. Uses separate materials cleaning for book shelves ____________

B. *Keeping Back the Materials*

1. Cleans the items used for cleaning ____________
2. Reports if new items are required ____________
3. Keeps back the items carefully in proper place ____________
4. Keeps an account of the items given for use ____________

TOTAL: ____________

3. Packing

A. Paper Packing

1. Gets appropriate cover ____________
2. Inserts books/papers ____________
3. Inserts the flap/closes with gum. ____________
4. Selects boxes/packing paper. ____________
5. Makes parcels and ties ____________

B. Cloth Packing

1. Arranges the materials in box ____________
2. Packs with packing paper ____________
3. Covers with cloth and stitches ____________
4. Gives for writing address ____________
5. Transferring materials ____________

4. Transferring Materials

A. Transfer When New Items Arrive

1. Finds place where the new items to store ____________
2. Cleans the places ____________
3. Takes out materials from vehicle ____________
4. Carries them and arrange ____________

B. Delivery of Items

1. Identifies various sections ____________
2. Follows instructions ____________
3. Carries items and gives ____________
4. Takes help whenever needed ____________

TOTAL: ____________

5. Photocopying

A. Operation of Photocopier

1. Connects the photocopier to the main supply ____________
2. Puts on the main switch ____________
3. Switches on the photocopier machine by pressing ON button ____________
4. Identifies the parts of the photocopier ____________
5. Recognizes the symbols/codes on the photocopier ____________

6. Keeps the white (Xerox) papers in appropriate tray __________
7. Takes the papers which are to be Xeroxed (originals) __________
8. Opens the upper cover of the machine __________
9. Keeps the paper to be Xeroxed in the appropriate place __________
10. Closes the upper cover __________
11. Sets the number (for number of copies) by pressing Appropriate buttons __________
12. Adjusts the codes for size (reduction and enlargement) __________
13. Operates the machine __________
14. Waits till the machine sets for operation __________
15. Sets the number of copies by pressing the number button __________
16. Takes out the Xeroxed copies __________
17. Checks the quality of the print __________
18. Rearranges the buttons for better quality print if necessary __________
19. Takes out the originals __________
20. Continues the activity till all the given papers are Xeroxed __________

B. *Setting and Stapling*

1. Counts the number of pages __________
2. Spreads the first set as per pages __________
3. Make sets by keeping paper's as per page __________
4. Staples __________
5. Opens and keeps staples if pins are over __________
6. Returns the sets of copies and originals __________

TOTAL: __________

II. Task Related Academics

A. *Reading Symbols and Numbers*

1. Aware of the name of equipments and materials used in library __________

2. Aware of the items used in cleaning ____________
3. Identifies the parts of photocopier ____________
4. Reads the symbols and numbers ____________
5. Identifies numbers for setting papers ____________
6. Can copy an address ____________

B. *Work Schedule*

1. Prepares the work schedule ____________
2. Follows the work schedule ____________
3. Reads the time and activities ____________

III. Safety Precautions

A. Occupational Safety

1. Takes care when handling fragile items ____________
2. Takes help while using machines ____________
3. Avoids hazardous environment ____________
4. Aware that books and papers to be handled gently ____________
5. Takes help when using chemicals especially for cleaning ____________
6. Returns the Xeroxed materials carefully ____________

TOTAL: ____________

B. Symptoms of Illness and Medication

1. Does not eat/drink non edible items ____________
2. Takes help while taking medicines ____________
3. Does not carry heavy weight which is above his capacity ____________
4. Reports the health problems to the supervisors ____________

Summative Evaluation Part—I

I. Main Tasks Areas *Dates:*____________

1. Setting furniture	7	____________
2. Cleaning book shelves	9	____________
3. Packing	9	____________
4. Transferring materials	8	____________

5. Photocopying	26	____________
TOTAL:	**59**	
II. Tasks Related Academics		*Dates:*____________
1. Reading symbols and numbers	6	____________
2. Work schedule	3	____________
TOTAL:	**9**	
III. Safety Precautions		*Dates:*____________
1. Occupation safety	6	
2. Symptoms of illness and medication	4	
TOTAL:	**10**	

Job Survey

The important activities involved in successful vocational rehabilitation are:

1. *Identify Potential Employment Opportunities*

1. Functionally assess the student.
2. Design an individualized vocational curriculum.
3. Select the most appropriate training experiences and placements with respect to the abilities and needs of the individual and the prospective employer.
4. Effectively instruct, using sound methodological procedures.

2. *Identifying Potential Employment Opportunities*

Job survey in the community would help to identify suitable jobs. The purpose of job survey is to list out potential employment opportunities and characteristic of the specific community in which individuals receiving training will initially seek jobs. Vocational trainers when deciding on the skills to target for training can use information gathered from the community assessment. It also assists to identify those skills required for performance on real jobs in actual employment sites.

Criteria for Identification of Jobs

- The unskilled jobs requiring minimum supervision, which

Individualizing the Transition Process

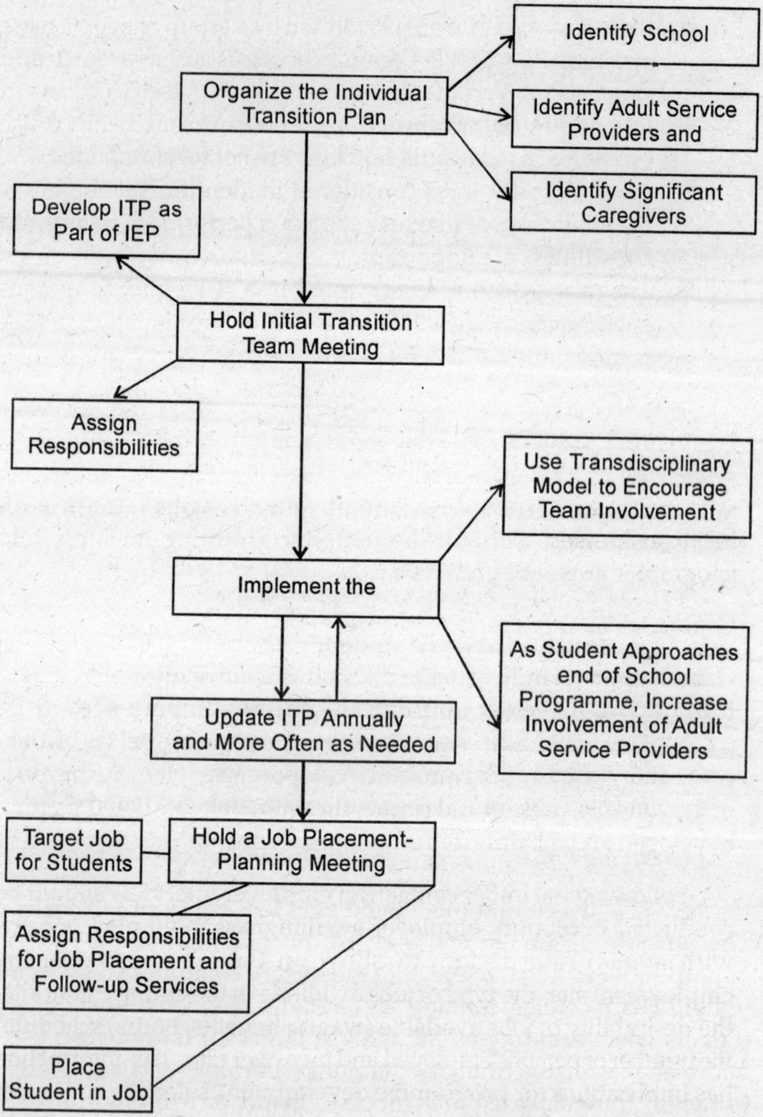

Figure 3: Individualizing the Transition Process

Source: McCarthy, P. *et. al.* (1985), Richmond, Virginia. School-to-Work Transition for Youth with Severe Disabilities, p. 37.

do not need assistance and do not involve risks, can be selected.

- If the unskilled jobs are performed by a group of people these jobs may be suitable because the necessary assistance and supervision is available within the group itself.
- Jobs, though simple by nature, if not performed, may cause problems in the production line, are not recommended.
- Another factor to be considered in identification of jobs is the environment in which the job is performed. Safety and friendliness are important.
- The jobs, which are performed in a risky and dangerous environment, may not be advisable for the mentally retarded persons due to the essential need of physical and mental alertness to safeguard oneself at the job site.

In order to effectively assess available jobs in the community, a systematic plan and procedure must be followed. The first step in systematically surveying a community involves generating a list of local businesses. This can be done by grouping business into geographic areas or by job type.

Contacting Employers

Once the list is complete, vocational programme developers should initiate contact with employers. Initial contacts should be introductory in nature. During initial contacts, the vocational counsellor/trainer/programme developer can explain the purpose of the contacts, present and future, the nature of vocational training developed and the time for future interactions.

Following the initial contact, an employer interview should be conducted to identify employer's willingness to employ persons with mental retardation, to allow on-the-job-training in the employment site, the type of jobs available in the employment site, the desirability of jobs available (wages, benefits, hours, schedule) the number of persons employed and turn over rate. This information has implications for programme development, selecting content of training, and making effective job matching for individual trainees. A file should be prepared for each business contacted and all relevant information should be kept for future reference when a trainer is making training or placement decisions for individual trainees.

Employer interviews help trainers to identify the jobs that are available and the desirability of jobs in the community. Additional information about the skills required to adequately performing a job in a specific business and the work related skills considered necessary for employment in the business should be obtained prior to establishing vocational training programmes. This information is directly related to curricular content of training programmes in specific jobs.

As per the report of the high power committee constituted by the Ministry of Social Justice and Empowerment, Government of India, to identify the jobs for the persons with disabilities in the private sector, 52 jobs were identified as shown in Table-1.

Table-1
Occupations Identified for Persons with Mental Retardation in Private Sector

S. No.	*N.C.O.*	*Occupation*	*Physical Requirements*
1.	351.90	Helpers in Stores	H, L, PP, S, SE, ST, W
2.	358.20	Peon, Office Boy	S, SE, ST, W
3.	399.40	Gummer Teleprinting	F, H, S, SE, RW
4.	430.30	Shop Assistant	F, S, SE
5.	450.10	Petrol Pump Salesman	F, H, SE, ST
6.	541.90	Sweeper, Cleaners and Related Workers	B, H, L, PP, S, SE, ST, W
7.	542.10	Water Carrier	H, L, SE, ST, W
8.	551.60	Presser Hand	B, L, SE, ST
9.	560.90	Saloon Boy	B, H, L, S, SE, ST
10.	640.24	Labourer (Plantation) (Nursery Worker, Plant Worker, Weeding Worker, Spraying Worker, Pickor/ Pucker)	B, PP, SE, ST, W
11.	641.35	Milk Dairy Attendant	B, F, PP, S, SE, ST, W
12.	651.10	Live Stock Worker	B, F, PP, SE, ST, W
13.	652.10	Gardener General	B, F, KC, SE
14.	752.90	Bobbin Cleaner	F, S, SE
15.	779.63	Bottling/Crowning	F, S, SE, ST
16.	782.20	Cigar or Cheroot Roller Helper	F, L, PP
17.	811.10	Carpenter, General	B, F, KC, S, SE, ST

(Contd.)

S. No.	*N.C.O.*	*Occupation*	*Physical Requirements*
18.	811.90	Carpenter, Helper	H, S, SE, ST, W
19.	812.90	Furniture Polisher	H, S, SE, ST, W
20.	819.45	Fret Saw Machine Operator	H, S, SE, ST, W
21.	819.35	Toy Maker, Wood	B, F, S, SE
22.	842.90	Assemblers, Other	B, F, S, SE, ST
23.	881.90	Jewellery Helper	B, F, S, OR ST, SE
24.	911.20	Envelope Maker	F, S, SE, ST
25.	921.10	Job Printer	F, P, S, SE
26.	922.20	Mono Operator	B, F, S, SE
27.	927.10	Book Binder	B, F, KC, PP, S, SE
28.	929.50	Silk Screen Painter	B, F, S, SE
29.	939.50	Painter Mate	B, F, PP, S, SE, W
30.	942.30	Caner	B, F, PP, S, ST
31.	949.58	Candle Maker	F, PP, S
32.	949.90	Card Board Box Maker	F, S, ST, SE
33.	959.20	White Washer	B, F, SE, ST
34.	963.20	Cleaner Motor Vehicle	B, F, SE, ST
35.	976.10	Packer, Hand (Carton Assemblers, Wooden Case Nailers)	B, F, S
36.	976.50	Packing Assistant	B, F, S, SE
37.	979.30	Liftman	S, SE, ST
38.	*	Photostat Machine Operator	F, L, S, ST
39.	*	CAD/CAM Programme Operator	F, L, SE
40.	*	Computer Accessory Assembler	F, S, SE
41.	*	Data Entry Operator	F, S, SE
42.	*	E-commerce Teller	F, S, SE
43.	*	E-commerce Accountant	F, S, SE
44.	*	Internet Server Administrator	F, S, SE
45.	*	Courier	L, S, SE, ST, W
46.	*	Plate Maker (Printing)	F, L, S, SE, ST, W
47.	*	Packing Machine	B, F, S, SE
48.	*	School Bus Attendant	H, SE, ST
49.	*	Diamond Cutter and Polisher	F, S, SE
50.	*	Canteen Attendant	F, H, S, SE, W

*= NCO numbers not available.

Abbreviations Used in the Lists of Occupations Physical Requirements

B	Work performed by Bending
F	Work performed by manipulating (with Fingers)

(Contd.)

H	Work performed by Hearing/speaking
KC	Work performed by Kneeling and couching
L	Work performed by Lifting
PP	Work performed by Pulling and pushing
S	Work performed by Sitting (on bench or chair)
SE	Work performed by Seeing
ST	Work performed by Standing
RW	Work performed by Reading and writing
W	Work performed by Walking

Vocational Assessment

Functional Vocational Assessment for Persons with Mental Retardation:

- Provides information on work readiness skills.
- Helps to identify suitable jobs in the community.
- Provides information on jobs selected.
- Identifies areas in which training is needed.
- Emphasizes on-the-job training.
- Evaluates work related skills and work behaviour.
- Targets employment for all trainees who are assessed.
- Extends support for job retention.

Assessment of Trainee Skills

There are two aspects in trainee's skills assessment as shown in the functional vocational assessment flowchart.

1. Generic assessment.
2. Specific skills assessment.

Generic skills are the pre-requisite skills/work readiness skills for a specific job selection and training. Generic skills include personal, social, academics domestic, safety, hand functioning and mobility skills. NIMH has developed an 80-item generic skills checklist to assess the pre-requisite skills. Based on the job selected, a criterion-referenced checklist can be developed for assessing the pre-requisite skills for specific job training.

Specific skills are the information gathered from the community assessment, interviews and job analysis.

The skills identified as required for success on community jobs should be the same skills on which trainees are assessed. Both work skills and work related skills should be considered in relationship to actual jobs available in the community. When trainees reach 18 years of age, vocational trainers should consider specific placements.

NIMH Vocational Assessment and Programming System (VAPS) has the following parts:

- Vocational Profile.
- Generic Skills assessment Check list.
- Job Analysis Format.
- Work Behaviour Assessment Check List.

Table-2

Functional Vocational Assessment Model

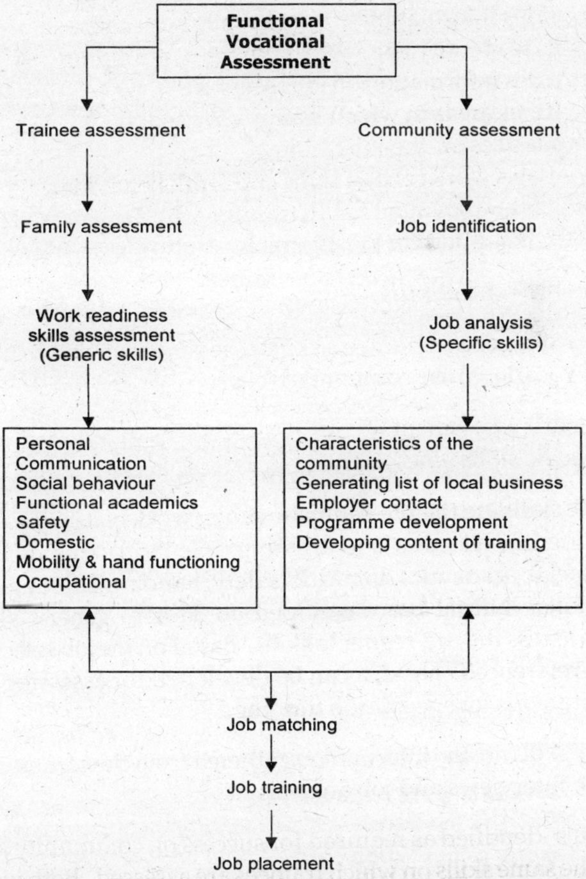

The Individualized Vocational Curriculum—Job Analysis

Selecting target skills (curriculum) for training should be a direct outcome of individual assessment procedures. The skills required of community employment sites comprise the curriculum for training. The job analysis consists of specific skills covering all areas of individualized vocational curriculum.

Job analysis is the plan used by employment trainers to ensure that employees are able to perform their jobs to the standard agreed to when negotiating with employers. Job analysis serves three major purposes.

1. It serves as the training plan for facilitating successful employment for the new employee.
2. It can be used as an accountability measure to ensure that the trainee's work is of highest quality possible.
3. It can be offered as a resource to the employer providing the job.

The Trainer's Objectives of Job Analysis are to

- develop an effective format for capturing all the components of the job that need to be trained.
- decide on a sequential process for performing the job analysis.
- perform the component steps of the job analysis process including:
- finalizing a comprehensive training plan based on all the information collected in the job analysis.
- developing the relationships and lines of communication with co-workers, supervisors, and the employer, which are necessary for the new employee to begin work.
- submitting a completed job analysis to the employer.

Job Analysis Format

Four useful categories when analyse a job site are:

1. Core work routine.
2. Episodic work routine.
3. Work behaviour
4. Work related skills.

1. *Core Work Routine*

Core work routines are those tasks that are likely to be the most frequently performed by the employee. Task analysis is the name typically given to the organization of the core work routines into teachable sequential steps. For most core routines, the job trainer chooses to provide direct systematic training to the employee. Any job restructuring, the employer should always approve adaptation or significant modification of a routine before it is implemented. Evaluation of worker performance on core routine occurs during training.

2. *Episodic Work Routines*

Episodic work routines occur infrequently for example two or three times per shift, once a day, or possibly even a few times per week. The organizational strategy for ordering the skills of an episodic routine is often referred to an inventory essentially the same as for a task analysis.

3. *Work Behaviour*

While conducting job analysis, the required behaviour expected to be successful on-the-job also should be listed out. Work behaviours necessary to continue on-the-job are punctuality, relationship with employer and co-workers, reaction to stress on different task, accuracy, speed, following instructions, ability to communicate and withstand fatigue.

4. *Work Related Skills*

Work related routines are not directly required by the employer for the job but they are vital for successful performance of the job. These routines may occur either on-site or off the job. An analysis of required work related skills may not always be possible through direct observation, since many of the skills required may not be easily observed at any given time. These skills include self-help, mobility and functional academics in addition to skills that relate to become a responsible worker.

Job Analysis Process

- Visit the job site.
- Observe the way in which current employees perform the various routines.

- Participate in the typical orientation procedures.
- Meet and get to know co-workers and supervisors.
- Have someone at the job site to teach you the routines.
- Perform the duties.
- Decide on the need for detailed job analysis and inventories for the various tasks of the job.
- Write task analysis.
- Obtain approval from the employer.
- Identify natural cues and consequences in the work routines of the employee.
- Select potential training strategies, motivating strategies, possible adaptations, and opportunities for job restructuring.
- Write a comprehensive training plan.
- Complete the job analysis form.

Set a starting date and communicate to the family members.

Guidelines for Employer Contacts

- Approach employers in a friendly and positive manner.
- Your interest and enthusiasm is a powerful persuader.
- Visit the employer at a convenient time.
- An employer may say "no" on the first visit, but depending on the impression you make, may be interested at a later time.
- Talk about the successful job retention and performance of workers with mental retardation and emphasize the positive characteristics of these workers.
- Tell the employer about the national awards for employing people with disabilities.
- Arrange to observe the work area so that you can analyze the job.

Vocational Training

Locating appropriate settings and materials for instruction are important factors for work experience training. To maximize generalization of skills, training sites should be carefully identified and selected to reflect the natural working conditions. Materials and equipments should be realistic and not simulated or artificially created.

Geographical proximity, wages, benefits, and work hours are additional variables that require special attention.

Training Setting

Once a vocational trainer becomes familiar with the community employment opportunities and the skills needed for gainful employment, he should consider the context in which trainees will be taught these skills. Both agency/school based and community based training options should be considered, depending upon the needs of the individuals to be served. However, all training environments should be designed to teach the jobs and skills identified as relevant in the community assessment.

Agency/School Based Training Sites

Any vocational training that is provided on property owned by an adult service agency or special school is considered agency/school based. Vocational trainers can simulate real jobs in these sites or provide experiences alongside actual agency/school employees.

Community Based Settings

Most trainees should receive training in community based vocational sites. The skills selected for training and the context in which those skills are taught must be carefully identified, based on a trainee's past experiences interests and skills. Community based options are training sites available in actual business in the community. These options can serve as vocational training and placement sites.

Combination of Community Based Training and Placement Sites

Combination of community based training and placement sites are those sites selected as a placement/employment site for one trainee and a training site for one or particular job type, as well as a future opportunity for paid employment for the trainee being so groomed. This type of community based option may provide vocational trainers with an alternative to one-to-one instruction for trainees being placed in jobs, and therefore, would require fewer staff across sites.

Considerations in Selecting Setting

The identification of appropriate vocational training settings for work experiences may require additional community assessment and cooperative planning among all special service personnel in the community. However, the need for careful planning should not be disregarded; generalization of skills is often difficult for persons with disabilities, thus emphasizing the importance of training in the most natural setting possible. As previously emphasized, the training sites should reflect the types of work that have been identified in the community as potential employment opportunities when conducting employer interviews during the community assessment process.

In developing and identifying potential training and placement settings, several issues should be discussed with the employer to ensure a more positive working relationship. Areas requiring specific attention and agreement include:

- Time schedule for training.
- How long the site will be used and how often.
- Space in which instruction can be provided.
- Specific job responsibilities that will be targeted as objectives and how the trainee's work performance will be coordinated with the normal work routine.
- Personnel responsible for training and supervision.
- Transport arrangements.

Written agreements should be developed that specify and document the conditions discussed with respect to any of these issues.

Training Methods

Once decisions regarding job experiences, target skills for instruction, and instructional settings have been made and a systematic assessment of an individual trainee's skills in relation to job requirements has been conducted, instruction can be initiated. Trainers should not expect trainees to acquire skills through exposure alone. Skills required to perform successfully on a job must be systematically taught to ensure that the trainee acquires and adequately performs those job skills.

Task analysis provides trainers with the content of instruction. Instructional procedures should be developed to guide trainers. Such procedures should identify:

- The stimuli desired to cue the target skills (e.g., natural cues such as work buzzers or artificial cues such as trainer instructions).

- The consequences that will be provided for correct responses (reinforcement).
- The procedures/prompts the trainer will use to facilitate correct performance of the task steps.
- The method the trainer will use to correct errors.
- Procedures the trainer will use for maintenance of the skill once it has been acquired.
- Procedures that will be used to facilitate generalization of skills to real work settings if trained initially in simulation.

Types of Employment

1. *Inclusive Employment*

Statement of International Labour Organization (ILO)

In the developing countries employment opportunities for persons with disabilities are extremely limited. Competition for jobs is great, as formal sector employment creation cannot keep pace with the growth in numbers of new job seekers entering the labour force. Wage and salary opportunities for persons with mental handicap, if available at all, are usually found in segregated sheltered workshops, offering low wages, poor working conditions, few prospects for advancement and limited social supports. Despite encouraging economic growth in many developing, countries, neither the formal employment sector, nor sheltered employment, is likely to offer wage or meaningful work opportunities for persons with mental handicap in the foreseeable future.

The ILO believes that the best opportunities for women and men with mental handicap in developing countries are the same as those for the working age population in general.

- Inclusive work in support of family farming,
- Household and productive activities, and
- Work in the fast growing informal sector of the economy.

The informal sector is creating more jobs and provides upwards of 80 per cent of employment in many developing economies. The informal sector is characterized by small-scale manufacturing and service activities which are organized informally, are unregulated, untaxed and offer no social protection. However, the informal sector offers ease of entry (no educational requirement, formal training qualification, letters of reference) to local income earning work opportunities to millions of men and women including individuals with mental handicap.

Inclusive work changes people, by increasing abilities, self-confidence, a sense of responsibility and independence. The dependent child of today can become an independent, productive adult of tomorrow, if given a chance to participate in work. Parents who protect their children with learning disabilities from the world of work, be it at home or in the community, do them a disservice and ensure their continued dependence. In developing countries, as elsewhere, the range of inclusive work opportunities for persons with mental handicap is limited only by our imagination, and courage to create choices.

Through inclusive work the family gains, the community gains, but above all, the individual with mental retardation gains.

2. *Competitive Employment*

Open employment in competitive situations is viewed as the entry of the individual into a normal work setting. The pay received should be at least minimum wage or at the prevailing wage rate for that specific job. Although initially there may be a need for some accommodation, once the task has been learned, the expectations and wage rates for the mentally retarded worker should not be different from normal worker.

The right to opportunity for competitive employment is a right which majority of persons with mental retardation has not received.

The capacity for competitive employment of significantly retarded persons is much greater than both professionals and parents have traditionally though. Educational and rehabilitative services in practice today do not yet reflect the ability of many persons with mental retardation to get a job and hold a job.

In India, three per cent government jobs are reserved for the persons with disability. Mentally handicapped people are not included under this reservation policy. The Ministry of Social Justice and Empowerment identified suitable jobs for persons with mental retardation in public sector. Similar exercise has been undertaken to identify jobs in the private sector also. Some arrangements are said to be officially made to include the disabled persons in the employment market both in public sector and private sector.

3. *Supported Employment*

Supported employment is an employment approach for individuals with mental retardation which enables them to be placed, trained, and supported in competitive jobs in integrated environment with the assistance of qualified persons. Individuals with mental retardation have repeatedly demonstrated the ability to master complex tasks in real jobs. Many have shown that they are able to perform meaningful work in community jobs and earn significant wages if given adequate support. These displays of competence show that people with severe disabilities can learn and perform competently. It also points to the need to provide work opportunities along with individualized job supports.

Evidence continues to mount that with special supported work services supplied by a job co.ıch at the place of employment, persons with mental retardation can experience much success in competitive employment.

Definition

"Supported employment is a paid employment for persons with developmental disabilities,
for whom competitive employment at or above the minimum wage in unlikely, and
who because of their disabilities need intensive ongoing support to perform
in a work setting, conducted in a variety of setting, particularly work sites in persons without disabilities are employed, supported by any activity needed to sustain paid work by persons with disabilities, including supervision, training and transportation."

U.S. Disability Act (1984)

Primary Features

- A focus on integrated employment.
- Priority given to people with disability who need ongoing support.

- Emphasis on productivity and wages.
- Availability of ongoing employment support.
- Availability of organizational alternatives to make employment a reality.
- A focus on integration.

The Need for Supported Employment

- Persons with mental retardation will not be able to obtain real job without professional help.
- They need individualized approach to ensure job retention.
- The amount of nature of professional support will vary from person to person and of course will be influenced by nature of disability.
- The persons with severe disability are unable to transfer the skills learned in specific centres to real jobs.

Objectives

- To employ persons with mental retardation in an integrated employment setting with reasonable wages and benefits.
- To provide appropriate training with ongoing support to maintain employment.
- To increase the number of persons with mental retardation in integrated employment setting at commensurate wages.
- To create an awareness among employers and co-workers on the capability of persons with mental retardation to perform the duties of the job in an integrated set up.

4. *Various Supported Employment Models*

(a) The Supported Work Model

The supported work model is one method of obtaining competitive employment for individuals with mental retardation. The specific steps in implementing the supported work model include job placement, job site training and advocacy, ongoing assessment and follow-up.

Job Placement: Job placement is comprised of several steps including employer's orientation, assessing the job sites, matching the job needs to the job trainee's potential, encouraging parent support, working out transport facilities and benefits.

Job placement is based on an accurate assessment of job requirements. This process has been referred to job analysis. It provides information about specific job routines, job related skills and behaviours.

Job placement often takes place with clients who do not have all the necessary works or social skills for immediate job placement. Skills training is provided after the client is placed on a job. The supported work model unlike the transitional placement process, does not require the client to be "job ready".

A job coordinator handles travel training, job interviews and other factors during the job placement process.

Job Site Training and Advocacy: The experiences in job site training in placement using support work model indicate that it is essential to train both specific skills and adjustment to the work environment. This involves training skills using behavioural techniques and advocating on the trainees behalf.

The application of reinforcement principles, manipulation of antecedent stimulus conditions, and use of co-workers as peer trainers require greater attention.

Advocacy is another important feature of the supported work model.

Orientation to the new job might involve locating toilet facilities, canteen, working out communication problems between trainee and co-workers and guiding the client in general work behaviours.

Ongoing Assessment: The third component of the model, ongoing assessment, marks a major difference between supported work and more traditional models of rehabilitation. Once a placement is made, client's feedback on the performance of the workers with mental retardation needs to be obtained so as to ascertain the gaps for better performance. This is done through supervisor evaluation data which are most effective, but verbal feedback may suffice. The quality of assessment is related to the ability of the client, staff available for data collection, and the specific need to evaluated certain problems.

Follow-up: Follow-up can include regular on-site visits, interacting with the employers, periodic reviews of supervisor evaluations, client progress reports, and parent's evaluation. Since person with mental retardation are immediately at risk of losing their jobs in competitive environment, follow-up support is imperative to ensure continuity on the job.

(b) Supported Jobs Model

The Supported Jobs Model is intended for individuals with severe disabilities typically served in a work activity centre or day activity centre. The model is designed for individuals expected to require intensive initial training and regular ongoing support and assistance on the job in order to maintain integrated employment.

Individuals who can be employed include those with little expressive language and adequate social behaviour. Support for individuals begins as continuous one-to-one on the job training, and fades to about one hour of support daily within a few months.

This model is composed of systems that cover all operations and management procedures. These systems include marketing, employer agreements, job matching training, management and integration.

Marketing: A business implementing the supported jobs model engages in concerted efforts to develop employment opportunities. Support organization must use an effective marking approach which sells the services of the agency and the skills of the employees with disabilities to prospective business. Marketing procedures provided by the model include.

- Market analysis which supplies relevant information about the local job market.
- Strategies for sales that make the sales efforts more successful by defining useful approaches for contacting local businesses and selling the organization's services.
- Job feasibility studies which allow for timely assessment of the appropriateness of a business for employing a person with moderate or severe disabilities.

Employment Agreements: Agreements are signed with businesses in one of two ways: as a service contract with the support organization, or for the business to directly hire the individual. Both contracts provide for the training and ongoing support of the employee, as well as monetary compensation. With the service contract, the business is invoiced for work done plus a percentage to cover taxes and benefits. The disabled individual is essentially an employee of the service organization.

Individual Job Match: The supported jobs model provides procedures to gather information on both potential job sites and the individuals who may be placed which can increase the likelihood of a successful individual-job match while minimizing the potential of denying employment to individuals who are too easily overlooked because of slow work rates or lack of skills. The assessments measure variables which directly affect the needs of the jobs and the individual, such as strength or endurance requirements, providing information relevant to a sound and fair match. Additionally, information is gathered on the type of work the person would like to do, and steps are taken to secure such a job.

Jobs are located in a variety of businesses within the community. Employment positions are usually four to six hours of daily work. Employees are not required to work at the productivity level of their non-handicapped peers. Jobs are sought that do not have time constraints and which do not require employees to bussing tables in a busy restaurant during breakfast. This is done so as not to exclude individuals with severe intellectual disabilities who are not expected to work at full productivity in the foreseeable future.

Training in Community Settings: Procedure for training in community settings involves an application of direct one-to-one instruction within the confines of businesses which limit both environmental control and the range of possible interventions. The supported jobs model provides procedure enable the support organizations and get trainer's maximum efficiency in identifying and training the job duty and social skills needed for successful job performance. Specific procedures provided by the model include:

- Teaching work and social behaviour.
- Self-monitoring to maintain performance.
- Training for infrequent and variable job demands.
- Fading the trainer.

Integration: The supported jobs model emphasizes integration in both individual job sites and in the surrounding community. Jobs are selected which provide a high degree of integration opportunities. Individuals participate in all socially interactive aspects of the job including staff meetings or parties. Additionally, employees are trained to use facilities, such as restaurants or stores, which are in close proximity to their place of employment. Social skills are imparted which foster successful social interaction.

Organizational Management: The support organization must be efficient in order to provide the training and support needed for successful job performance by the individuals served. The supported jobs model provides procedures for the creation of the support organization, satisfying external regulating agency requirements, maintaining sensible staffing patterns, maintaining financial stability and projecting an appropriate business image.

(c) The Mobile Crew Model

The Mobile Crew Model is designed for small communities and rural areas but may operate in a large city. The crew or crews each have up to five individuals with moderate to severe intellectual disabilities, and one supervisor. Mobile Crews tend to operate out of a van. The Mobile Crew Model provides procedures for operating the crew as a business to generate wages for the workers. The model also provides procedures for the training and support of individuals with disabilities.

(d) The Enclave Model

In Enclave model a small group of persons with disabilities (about six persons) is employed in an industry and receives continual support by the vocational staff. Creative enclave models do not cluster the persons with disabilities together, but rather facilitate placement of individuals throughout the work plant. Support is typically more intense in this model. Support is also systematic, continuous and reliable. Workers are either paid by the business at a rate of at least minimum wage. Integration is achieved by facilitating interactions among employees at break times, lunch times, before and after work, and through work related interactions.

(e) The Bench Work Model

The Bench Work Model is a comprehensive set of procedures for training and employing people with disabilities within a facility-based-programme engaged in benchwork assembly jobs. The model is organized to achieve the goals of community based supported employment, competence in performing non-vocational activities, and maximized productivity and earnings. The Benchwork Model includes specific procedures related to each of four critical components: management and finance, commercial operations, training and habilitation information and evaluation.

(f) Apprenticeships

In this model, a person with disability serves as an apprentice or helper to a skilled person. The person may be employed in a printing press, canteen, or in various similar trades. The unique feature is that the individual works with one or two skilled individuals and assists in the performance of the particular trade. The person is given on-the-job training by the skilled person. Wages are usually no less than minimum wage and the individual is employed by the business.

(g) Small Enterprise

In this model, a small business is established. Within the small business about six disabled people work with non-disabled people. The small business operates like any business, generating work and paying employees from revenues received. The small enterprise is located within the community to enhance opportunities for integration. Successful small business encourage integration within its work force as well as with other merchants and business.

Benefits of Supported Employment

- Persons with mental retardation get an opportunity to work in an integrated set-up.
- It helps them to engage themselves in productive work that has real value in economy.
- It produces income which creates new opportunities for community participation.
- The employer is able to pay on the basis of productivity, so that labour cost per unit of work remains same.
- It gives social benefits.
- It offers the opportunity for persons with mental retardation to become self-supporting.

Supported Employment Models

APPRENTICESHIPS

- Serves as an apprentice or helper to skilled persons.
- Not less than minimum wage.
- The individual is employed by the business.

ENCLAVES IN INDUSTRY

- Ongoing support in an industry-based-programme sponsored by a host business.
- May or may not be minimum wage.
- Level of integration may vary.

SUPPORTED WORK MODEL

- Ongoing support.
- Individual job placement and training.
- Minimum or above minimum wage.
- High integration.

Results of Transition

SUPPORTED JOBS MODEL

- Ongoing support.
- Individual job placement and training.
- Sub-minimum wage.
- High integration.

SPECIALIZED BUSINESS/ SMALL ENTERPRISE

- Ongoing support.
- Specialized sub-contract work or other small business venture.
- Intensive systematic training.
- Sub-minimum wages.

MOBILE WORK CREWS

- Ongoing support.
- Small mobile business, which must be based on community labour needs.
- May or may not be minimum wage.
- Level of integration may vary.

5. *Sheltered Employment*

Sheltered workshop provides non-competitive long-term employment to persons with mental retardation. Its uniqueness lies in its ability to provide them with an opportunity to make a useful contribution to society and to their own well-being through productive work.

Definition

A work oriented rehabilitation facility, with a controlled working environment and individual's vocational goals, which utilizes work experience and related services for assisting the handicapped person to progress towards normal living and a productive vocational status.

– *Association of Rehabilitation Facilities*

Here the term "controlled working environment" refers to the fact that the work is done under the supervision of a trained staff, and that the setting is adapted to the special needs and limitations of the workers.

The "related services" are directed toward the goal of total rehabilitation and include medical, psychological and social services designed to protect the client and to assist with personal problems.

Objectives

The main objective of the sheltered employment is to prepare the persons with mental retardation for competitive employment or to provide a terminal sheltered job.

It is not possible for all trainees to achieve these goals and for this reason sheltered workshops are designed to serve two types of clients.

1. The severely disabled individuals who can profit from intensive training, adjust to the work situation and develop a certain level of skills and productivity to enter labour market.
2. The severely disabled person who accepts the work situation and develops some skill and productivity, but is unable to meet the requirements of the open labour market.

Sheltered workshops provide both occupational training and remunerative employment opportunities for persons with mental retardation.

Characteristics

Payne and Pattern in 1981 described several common characteristics of sheltered workshops.

- Employees usually work on contractual jobs.
- These contract jobs are usually of short duration, therefore a staff person is needed to bring in new jobs.
- Most tasks are broken into small steps.
- Jobs usually proceed in an assembly line fashion, one part is added at each step of the process until a final product is completed.
- The facility may or may not provide vocational assessment and training for persons outside the centre.

Advantages

The benefits offered by the sheltered workshop are many and varied.

- The experience increases the person's self-respect and self-esteem by offering an opportunity to make a useful social contribution.
- It provides a work setting that is especially adapted to individual need and limitations, under the guidance of specialists not only in vocational training but also in total situation.
- It exposes the handicapped person to many demands and discipline found in a real work situation.
- It gives an opportunity to test personal ability and adaptability in a better atmosphere before venturing into competitive employment.
- The individual not only works under the supervision of vocational experts, but has the added benefit of receiving care from related services.

Organizing the Workshop

- The selection and organization of a board of Directors to be responsible for formulating the overall policy determining the programme, evaluating community needs and resources, interpreting workshop activities to the public, obtaining financial support, selecting and giving general direction to the executive director.
- Establishing criteria for the client in terms of age, type and severity of disability and location of residence. A decision must be made as on whether the workshop will serve the client with a single disability or different disabilities together.
- Getting registered as per the Societies/Trust Act.

- Finding a location for the physical plant.
- Staffing the workshop.
- Drawing up an estimated budget to be presented to the community to gain its financial support, since the workshop cannot be self-supporting and will need to be subsidized.
- Establishing record-keeping and accounting practices.
- Public relation plan designed to build community confidence in the workshop.

Workshop Programme

Stage 1: *Intake Process*,

In this process a qualified rehabilitation worker collects information about the person with mental retardation in various aspects like medical, psychological, social, education and vocational. On the basis of the information collected, a complete case record is constructed for the double purpose of planning the rehabilitation programme and charting progress of the person with mental retardation.

Stage 2: *Work Tryout*

In this stage the qualified rehabilitation worker devices a work programme designed to evaluate physical capacities, learning ability, special aptitudes and skills and ability to maintain social relationships and meet demands required by work situation. The tryout may include office work, service activities, packaging, production and machine operation. During this period the person with mental retardation is observed and assessed for the ability to follow directions. The qualified rehabilitation worker and person with mental retardation together determine vocational objectives and if the person with mental retardation has been previously employed whether training should be focused on a modified version of former occupation or a new occupation.

Stage 3: *Work Conditioning and Training*

This stage is long for the person with mental retardation to learn a specific job and if necessary, develop skills that will compensate for personal limitations. During this period the person with mental retardation is instructed in the use of tools and equipments and receives training in the economical use of raw materials, manipulative skills and coordination, industrial safety and concepts of time, spatial relationships and money value as needed.

Stage 4: *Job Placement*

The person with mental retardation is ready to take a job in competitive industry or extended employment. The job counsellor identifies a job for the person and places him on the job.

Stage 5: *Follow-up*

The counsellor keeps in touch with the person with mental retardation in order to evaluate progress, to make sure that a satisfactory adjustment is taking place.

During the entire process the workshop experiences are reinforced by supportive services, particularly medical and psychological. The objectives is to help the person with mental retardation build a positive self image, overcome tendencies towards over dependency and over sensitivity, and adapt more fully to the world of work by improving work habits, personal appearance, social skills and adjust to special demands such as time, pressure, noise and discipline of training.

Criticisms

Some of the criticisms against the sheltered workshop model are:

- Few persons with mental retardation move onto competitive employment.
- The persons with mental retardation attending sheltered workshop often get very low wages which is ascribed to their low productivity.
- It was seen that the productivity of workers whether handicapped or not, is highly dependent on the efficiency of the productivity process and the value that society places on what is produced.
- If the number of person with mental retardation is less, it is difficult to accept large sub-contracts which in turn affects its productivity and profit.
- The small workshops have only limited variety of jobs. It is difficulty to place persons with mental retardation in various jobs that are suitable to their capabilities.

- Most workshops are restricted in their ability to employ efficient methods of production and skilled trainers.
- Many of these workshops are not in a position to match the productive efficiency of private firms. Very often, they lack capital, experience and technical knowledge it is difficult for them to find a wide market for the products.

6. *Group Employment*

Sheltered workshop has its own limitations to provide remunerative employment, parents and community interaction and overall personality development of the trainees. The group employment is modified version of sheltered employment. It is organized by the group of parents or an adult service providing agency. It provides vocational skill training, remunerative employment, community interaction and personality development of persons with mental retardation. All categories of persons with mental retardation in small groups are engaged in productive activities on commercial line which brings profit out of which the special employees an supervisors are paid.

When the special employees find better opportunities, they gradually move towards open and supported self-employment. Others continue in the production centres which provide group employment and job related activities.

Objectives of Group Employment

- To promote remunerative employment for persons with mental retardation.
- To crate awareness and utilize the maximum capabilities of persons with mental retardation.
- To involve parents and community in the vocational rehabilitation services.
- To facilitate transition from group employment to open/ self-employment.
- To engage the persons with moderate and severe mental retardation in economically useful activities.

Organization of Group Employment

Stage 1: *Formation of Registered Group*

- Collect the data of adult persons with mental retardation above 15 years of age, residing with a radius of 5 to 8 kms.

- Invite the parents of the identified persons with mental retardation and conduct a programme.
- Get them registered as a group under the Indian Society's Registration Act.

Stage 2: *Assessment*

- Functionally assess the identified persons with mental retardation.
- Identify the products which can be manufactured at a commercial line and marketing facilities.
- Prepare job analysis.

Stage 3. *Setting-Up Production Centre*

- Procure necessary machinery, equipments and raw materials.
- Select initial training with the support of parents, siblings and volunteers.

Stage 4: *Large Scale Production*

- Check quality and quantity
- Maintain proper accounts
- Start payment to the employees and supervisors.
- Check periodically, add more products and modify the process if necessary.

NIMH has initiated and promoted group employment model throughout India. About 18 production centres, organized with the technical and financial support of NIMH and currently continuing successfully in different parts of the country.

Benefits

The organizers of group employment listed the benefits they gained out of their venture. Some of the benefits are:

- The persons with mental retardation and parents gained self-confidencee.
- Parents interaction improved.
- The persons with mental retardation found a place to work and earn.
- They became contributing members of family and society.

- They achieved work skills and work behaviour.
- A sense of responsibility and a feeling to togetherness developed.
- Community resources were tapped.

Problems

The difficulties faced by the organizers are given below:

- Problem of marketing the products.
- Financial constraint.
- Lack of time for organizers.
- Lack of entrepreneurship.

The benefits for the persons with mental retardation are much more than the problems the organizers faced. The model is spreading in India.

The most critical aspects of an individual's capacity for employment are:

Parental Support,
A Friendly and Social Personality
and
A Desire to Work

Notice that I.Q scores, test scores, or academic abilities are not necessarily important features of the successfully employed persons with mental retardation.

7. *Self-Employment/Self-Directed Employment as an Option for Inclusion*

Definition

Self-directed employment refers to work situations where people with disabilities, to a significant degree, have a prime decision-making role with respect to the kind of work that is done, how time is allocated, what kinds of investment in time and money should be made, and how to allocate revenue generated (Neufeldt, 1998).

While self-employment is the most frequent expression of self-directed employment, whether part or full time, it may also refer to group approaches such as worker owned business. The term was coined as a way of describing income generation strategies of people with disabilities in an international study of 41 countries (Neufeldt and Albright, 1998).

Interest in self-directed employment has been growing in developing countries since 1981 according to the study. The growing interest can be explained in part by the relatively few salaries jobs available, and in part by the absence of publicly funded income support programmes. Countries such as Jamaica, Philippines, Thailand and Zimbabwe, amongst others, have accumulated a considerable wealth of experience in ways to systematically support the development of self-directed employment by people with disabilities.

What work can an individual with a mental handicap do at home or in the informal sector in a developing country?

Inclusive Work Opportunities at Home

There are many ways that a family member with mental handicap, according to his or her ability, can contribute productively to the maintenance of the household. Such activities vary according to the location where one resides (rural area, town, city, urban) and include:

- Helping with daily chores – gathering wood, carrying water, food preparation, cleaning laundry, taking care of children.
- Helping with productive activities of the family – farming and gardening (preparing land, weeding, protecting against birds and animals, harvesting, food storage), taking care of animals, fishing.
- Helping with household income – generating activities – laundry, poultry, making of handicrafts, food items (preserves, snacks, butter, cheese), other products for sale.

Inclusive Work Opportunities in the Community

Many youth and adults with mental handicap can acquire vocational skills through apprenticeship and work experience and can participate productively as a paid worker in informal sector manufacturing or service activities, including:

- Helping with preparation and clean-up work related to small-scale manufacturing activities – wood work, metal work, leather tanning, cloth dyeing, food processing and so on.

- Helping with the packing or packaging of products – fruits, vegetables, eggs, flowers, manufactured items, etc.
- Helping with work related to the provision of services such as bicycle, auto, etc.

Gaining sufficient training and experience, persons with mental retardation can organize self-employment programmes related to the above mentioned work opportunities in the community with family support.

Requirements for Self-Employment Schemes

Professional Help: Professional's role comes in providing expertise regarding how to train, the techniques and strategies to be used in training in providing follow-up services in giving necessary details regarding availability facilities etc. Vocational guidance is important.

Financial Aspects: The monetary aspects like raising capital, finding buyers for products, etc., are to be considered, especially, while initiating production units.

Parental Role: As persons with multiple disabilities may not be fully independent, some amount of support in terms of organization, decision-making, budgeting, etc., has to be provided by parents and others.

Advantages of Self-Employment

- It is community based, habilitation becomes a natural process.
- It saves complications involved in open/supported employments like acceptability by co-workers, employers etc.
- It is cost-effective. It makes use of available materials and opportunities in the society.
- Gives a sense of responsibility and self-esteem to persons with disabilities.

Agriculture

Agricultural Work Offers Many Advantages

- *Physical activity:* Due to over-protection or neglect, many retarded adolescents and adults are in very poor physical condition. Physical activity involved in agricultural work improves fitness, co-ordination, morale and allows for group interaction.

- *A healthy environment:* Agricultural activities provide fresh air and sunshine.
- *Aesthetic sense:* Working with tender plants, colourful flowers, scenic landscape, helps to cultivate a sense of appreciation towards nature.
- *Mobility:* The nature of the work allows, and often calls for, a good amount of moving around, which is generally advantageous.
- *Variety:* Agricultural work usually provides more diversity on a daily and seasonal basis than in the case with semi-skilled employment in the cities.

Funds

State and Central Governments have schemes to provide financial assistance for persons with disability. The National Handicapped Finance and Development Corporation (NHFDC) has been incorporated by Ministry of Welfare, Government of India on 24th January, 1997 under Section 25 of the Companies Act, 1956 as a company not for profit. It is wholly owned by Government of India and has an authorized share capital of Rs. 400 crores (Rupees four hundered crores only).

The Main Objectives of NHFDC are:

- Promote economic development activities for the benefit of the persons with disabilities.
- Promote self-employment and other ventures for the benefit/ economic rehabilitation of the persons with disabilities.
- Assist individuals with disabilities or groups of individuals with disabilities by way of loans and advances for economically and financially viable schemes and projects.

NHFDC Schemes to Promote Self-Employment Amongst Persons with Mental Retardation, Cerebral Palsy and Autism

Persons with mental retardation, cerebral palsy or autism may not be eligible to seek loan and enter into a legal contract. In such cases following categories of persons are eligible for financial assistance from NHFDC.

- Parents of dependant mentally retarded persons.
- Spouse of dependant mentally retarded persons.

Persons seeking loan from NHFDC under this category should encourage self-employment of the mentally retarded persons. Projects should be identified in such a way that there is direct involvement and participation of the beneficiary in the projects.

Indicative areas for financing are:

(i) Shop or store
(ii) Assembling unit
(iii) Workshop or repair shop
(iv) Envelop making unit
(v) Pickle, papad, wadi making unit
(vi) Home unit for making squash, jam etc.
(vii) Bakery
(viii) Xerox Centre
(ix) Tailoring unit
(x) DTP centre
(xi) Screen printing
(xii) Poultry
(xiii) Dairy farming
(xiv) Horticulture
(xv) Handloom unit
(xvi) Block, textile printing

Maximum loan available under this scheme is Rs. 2.5 lakhs.

Eligibility Criteria

(a) Criteria of Disability

In order to be eligible for loans on concessional interest rates from the Corporation, the minimum degree of disability shall not be less than 40 per cent (IQ below 70).

(b) Economic/Income Criteria

Unemployed disabled persons whose family income is below Rs. 80,000 p.a. for rural areas and Rs. 1,00,000 p.a. for urban areas (two times of poverty line) are eligible for availing loan facility. ('family' means parents or spouse of dependent disabled).

Minimum age limit for availing loan is 18 years and maximum age is 55 years. However, the maximum age could be relaxed in the case of professionally qualified entrepreneurs.

The sanctioned loan amount and repayment period will depend on the age of applicant.

Rate of Interest

Sl. No.	Loan Amount	Interest by NHFDC	Interest by (Channelizing Agency)	Total
1.	Loan amount less than Rs. 50,000	3%	2%	5%
2.	Loan amount above Rs. 50,000 and upto Rs. 1,00,000	4%	2%	6%
3.	Loan amount above Rs. 1,00,000 and upto Rs. 5,00,000	7%	2%	9%
4.	Loan amount above Rs. 5,00,000	8%	2%	10%

Other Requirements

The applicant:

1. should be an Indian Citizen.
2. should be domicile of the state where the project is proposed to be put up.
3. should have relevant educational/technical/vocational qualification/experience/background.
4. should not have any large outstanding debt from other organization and should not be financial defaulter.
5. should be from agricultural background and project location should be in agricultural area if seeking loan under the scheme 'Assistance for Agricultural Activities'.

- For women with disability, a rabate of 2 per cent on interest is provided.
- A rebate of 0.5 per cent on interest is provided for timely repayment of loan.

Recovery of Loan

(a) The entire loan shall be repaid within a reasonable period but not exceeding 7 years including the moratorium period. The repayment shall be on half yearly/quarterly/monthly basis. For agriculture and horticulture projects repayment shall be on yearly basis. The repayment period will be worked out during appraisal and sanction of scheme on the basis of income potential of the proposed project.

(*b*) A suitable moratorium period depending on the merit and requirement of the project will be allowed.

(*c*) A rebate of 0.5 per cent on interests is provided for timely payment of all installment.

(*d*) A penal interest of 3 per cent will be charged from channelizing agency for default in timely repayment. The channelizing agency will also charge penal interest of 3 per cent from the beneficiary for default in repayment.

The prospects for success of self-employment is enhanced if the person has a concept of themselves as wanting to run their own business, if the person has or can acquire the skills necessary for their particular line of business, if supports such as small loans funding, business consultation and monitoring services are available and if the person has a strong personal support network.

Few Projects Suggested Under NHFDC

S.No.	*Tasks Persons with Mental Retardation Can Perform*
1. ***Textiles and Related Industries***	
■ Textile projects ■ Knitted products ■ Carpet and rug products ■ Rope and twine products ■ Dress products ■ Leather products	■ Spinning ■ Dyeing ■ Lace-making ■ Weaving ■ Knitting ■ Embroidering ■ Making handbags ■ Making belts ■ Making nets ■ Stitching buttons
2. ***Wooden and Related Industries***	
■ Textile projects ■ Furniture products ■ Cane products ■ Building fixtures ■ Paper products	■ Cutting ■ Shaping ■ Fitting ■ Assembling ■ Repairing ■ Greasing and oiling ■ Cleaning ■ Tool assembling ■ Caning furniture

(Contd.)

S.No.		Tasks Persons with Mental Retardation Can Perform
		■ Making baskets ■ Making brushes
3.	**Household and Cottage Industries**	
	■ Candle production ■ Match production ■ Pickle production ■ Papad production ■ Agarbathi production ■ Rope production ■ Dolls production ■ Gunny bag production ■ Book binding ■ Paper cup/plate production ■ Leaf cup/plate production	■ Boiling ■ Pouring into moulds ■ Cutting ■ Pasting ■ Dipping ■ Rolling ■ Packing ■ Twisting ■ Kneading ■ Mixing ■ Blending

S.No.		Tasks Persons with Mental Retardation Can Perform
	■ Bleaching and dyeing ■ Cane and bamboo products ■ Baskets ■ Coir products ■ Soap making ■ Hand made paper	■ Stitching ■ Operating pressing machine ■ Sewing
4.	**Laundering Services**	
	■ Bleaching and dyeing ■ Launderer helper ■ Presser helper ■ Machine attendant dry cleaner	■ Laundering by hand ■ Pressing by hand ■ Operating machines ■ Drying clothes ■ Folding clothes ■ Hanging clothes ■ Packaging
5.	**Hair Dressing Services**	
	■ Barber attendant ■ Beautician attendant	■ Sweeping barber shop ■ Dusting hair ■ Replacing used linen ■ Cleaning tools

"I am proud of my son", this is what Naimathulla's father said, when he was given the National Award as a Best Special Employee in the category of mental retardation during the year 1998.

Naimathulla had two mentally retarded brothers. One of them passed away. His father was very much disturbed due to the three sons with mental retardation in his family. When Aakanksha, a production centre for the persons with mental retardation was started in the railway campus by the parents of the mentally retarded children of Railway Employees, Naimathulla joined the centre and learned to make stationary materials. After the working hours, he used to work at his grandfather's public telephone booth. Exposure to various job opportunities helped him to realize his potentials. Later, he left the production centre and started working in a screen-printing unit. Thus, he became a full time worker in the telephone booth and screen-printing unit for which he was awarded as the best employee in the category of persons with mental retardation.

Naimathulla is a good athlete. He had a chance to go to USA, for the International Special Olympics and he won a gold medal. In any special occasion, he proudly wears the jacket which he got during the International Special Olympics and shares his experience.

Naimathulla was felicitated during the National Special Employees Meet at NIMH, for receiving National Award. He tells his friends that everybody should work and earn their living and stand on their own feet. He is a role model to others.

Unit Summary

- Mental retardation is a disability characterized by significant limitation both in intellectual functioning and in adaptive behaviour. This disability originates before age 18.

- Within an individual, limitations often co-exist with strengths.
- With appropriate personalized supports over a sustained period, the life functioning of the person with mental retardation generally will improve.
- Transition, the process of moving from one setting to another, is one of the most important aspects of rehabilitation. It requires professionals and parents to redefine the roles and responsibilities of school and adult service providers.
- Transition is a carefully planned process from school to work, which should be developed and implemented for students with disabilities who have only three years remaining in school.
- An individual transition plan should be initiated by school personnel or adult service providers and involve special and vocational educators, vocational rehabilitation counsellors, parents, the student and employers.
- Transition may be viewed as a four-step process:
  1. Systematic school instruction.
  2. Planning for transition.
  3. Placement in meaningful employment.
  4. Follow-up services.
- The transition team should include professionals representing special education, vocational rehabilitation, vocational education, developmental disabilities, social services, medical services, parents and employers from local business.
- A thorough and ongoing process of community analysis is used to identify jobs to develop a vocational curriculum, which reflects skills identified in the local community. Information gathered by the vocational trainer during community analysis enables the trainer to make decisions about the content of vocational curriculum.
- The ITP should include goals related to all aspects of work (e.g., job skills, transportation, handling money). It may be a portion of the student's Individual Education Plan (IEP). Updates of the ITP should coincide with the annual IEP meeting while the individual is continuing in the school.

- The important aspects of successful vocational habilitation are: (1) Identifying potential employment opportunities, (2) Functionally assessing the student, (3) Designing an individualized vocational curriculum, (4) Selecting the most appropriate training experiences and placements with respect to the abilities and needs of the individual and the prospective employer, and effectively instructing, using sound methodological procedures.
- Employer interviews help trainers to identify the jobs that are available in the community. This information is directly related to curricular content of training programmes in specific jobs.
- The Functional Vocational Assessment Model has two parts: Community Assessment and Assessment of Trainee Skills. It targets employment for all trainees who are assessed. It selects the areas in which training is needed and emphasizes on-the-job training.
- Job analysis is the plan used by employment trainers to ensure that employees are able to perform their jobs to the standard agreed to when negotiating with employers. Job analysis serves three major purposes:
    1. It serves as the training plan for facilitating successful employment for the new employee.
    2. It can be used as an accountability measure to ensure that the trainee's work is of highest quality possible.
    3. It can be offered as a resource to the employer providing the job.
- Geographical proximity, wages, benefits and work hours are additional variables that require special attention.
- Important work behaviours are: Punctuality, relationship with peers, relationship with staff, reaction to stress on different task, physical capacity to do the task, acquisition of training, accuracy, speed, ability to follow instructions, ability to communicate, ability to withstand fatigue, independence, persistence and endurance.
- Competitive employment, supported employment, sheltered employment, and self-employment are four variations aimed at providing long-term employment for individuals with developmental disabilities.
- NHFDC provides funds for promoting self-employment among persons with disabilities.

Check Your Progress

Define the terms:

- Habilitation, rehabilitation, vocational rehabilitation.
- Explain the stages of vocational rehabilitation with a flow chart.
- Discuss the need for transition from school to work.
- What are the key elements of transition?
- Explain the steps to construct vocational curriculum.
- Discuss the guidelines for school based vocational training.
- Mention the criteria for job identification.
- Explain functional vocational assessment with a flow chart
- What are the objectives of job analysis?
- Explain the process of job analysis.
- What are the different types of employment?
- Write short notes on:
- Inclusive employment, Supported employment, Sheltered employment.
- Importance of self- employment.
- Schemes under NHFDC.

Assignment/Activities

- Conduct a job survey for persons with mental retardation.
- Prepare a vocational curriculum for a mildly retarded person studying at pre-vocational level.

Points for Discussion/Clarification

....

....

....

....

REFERENCES

1. Bellamy, G.T., Rhodes,L.E., Mank, D.M., and Albin, J.M.(1988), *Supported Employment: A Community Implementation Guide*. Baltimore: Brookes.
2. Mc Carthy, P. *et al.* (1985), *School-to-Work Transition for Youth with Severe Disabilities*, Virginia Common Wealth University, Richmond, Virginia, 23284-001.

3. *Mental Retardation, Definition, Classification and Systems of Support* (2002), American Association on Mental Retardation, Washington.
4. *National Handicapped Finance Developmental Corporation*, Government of India.
5. Rusch, F. and Mithaug, D.(1980), *Vocational Training for the Mentally Retarded Adults*, Champaign,IL: Research Press.
6. Thressiakutty, A.T. and Rao, G.L. (2001), *Transition of Persons with Mental Retardation from School to Work – A Guide, National Institute for the Mentally Handicapped*, Secunderabad.
7. Thressiakutty, A.T. and Rao, G.L. (2001), *Curriculum for Vocational Education, Transition of Persons with Mental Retardation from School* to Work, National Institute for the Mentally Handicapped, Secunderabad.
8. Thressiakutty, A.T. and Rao, G.L., (2003), *Curriculum for Vocational Education, Transition of Persons with Mental Retardation from School to Work*, National Institute for the Mentally Handicapped, Secunderabad.
9. Thressiakutty, A.T. and Rao, G.L. (2003), *Hope Beyond Hope – Some Success Stories*. National Institute for the Mentally Handicapped, Secunderabad.
10. Thressiakutty, A.T. and Rao, G.L. (2004), *Curriculum for Vocational Education, Transition of Persons with Mental Retardation from School* to work, National Institute for the Mentally Handicapped, Secunderabad.
11. Wehman, P. (1981), *Competitive Employment*, Baltimore: Brookes.
12. Wehman, P. Kregal, J., and Barcus, J.M. (1985), *From School to Work: A Vocational Transition Model for Handicapped Students*, Exceptional children, 52, 25-37.
13. Wolfensberger, W. Nirje, B. Olshansky, S., Perske, R. and Roos, P. (1972), *The Principle of Normalization in Human-Services*. Toronto: National Institute on Mental Retardation.
14. Thressiakutty, A.T. (1998), *Functional Vocational Assessment and Programming System*, National Institute for the Mentally Handicapped, Secunderabad.

UNIT–4

Social Skills Required at Various Developmental Stages Suited to Occasions – Social Competencies Required for Independence Living in Persons with Mental Retardation

STRUCTURE

- Introduction
- Objectives
- The Need for Social Skill Training
- When to Start Training?
- What to Train?
- How to Train?
- Unit Summary
- Check Your Progress
- Assignment/Activities
- Points for Discussion/Clarification
- Reference

4

Social Skills Required at Various Developmental Stages Suited to Occasions—Social Competencies Required for Independence Living in Persons with Mental Retardation

Introduction

Appropriate social behaviours are necessary for any person to be an acceptable member of the society. Every human being is expected to follow certain standards of social behaviour, set by the society according to the cultural norms and age level of the individuals.

In case of mentally persons, intensive training is needed to cultivate appropriate social behaviours. Instead of keeping them away from the society, giving them chances to mix in the society from the childhood itself will lead them towards gaining social competency. The training should be started very early in life. The family, the relatives, neighbours, friends, and the society at large are responsible for the social skills training of the persons with mental retardation.

Objectives

After studying this unit, the students will be able to

- understand the need for social skills training.
- identify the necessary social skills required for people with mental retardation at various stages.
- learn the methods of social skills training at home in the school and the community.

The Need for Social Skill Training

- Normal children learn social skills as they grow. In case of children with mental retardation, the more the chances for training and exposure to social situations, the better they learn the skills.
- If they are not trained, usually they will be left in the house and be deprived of outings and participating in social functions.
- If they are able to behave appropriately in a group situation, they will be accepted by the group.

When to Start Training?

- A mentally retarded individual needs stimulation, repeated chances, supervision and training to develop proper skills.
- Social skill training should be started as early as possible in his/her life.
- During infancy the child should get maximum stimulation from the family members. The family members should talk to the child whenever possible, even if he/she does not talk.
- During childhood, give him chances to play with other children.
- Continue the training through adolescence and adulthood in necessary social skills.

What to Train?

- Use the activity checklist for social skill training. After checking what he can do, select the activities which are most important in daily life and start training in those specific activities. 15 items related to social skills have been selected and tips are given for training. The second unit in part 2 explains the higher level social skills to be trained at adolescent and adult stages. The following skills are explained in this unit:

1. Waits for needs to be fulfilled
2. Plays with peers sharing objects
3. Greets others
4. Obeys Commands
5. Says 'Please', 'Thank you', 'Sorry' appropriately
6. Helps parents in household tasks

7. Asks permission
8. Takes turn
9. Participates appropriately at meal time
10. Dresses and grooms appropriate to the situation
11. Visits relatives and friends
12. Participates in social functions
13. Behaves appropriately with the opposite sex
14. Returns borrowed materials
15. Identifies human service persons and community helpers

Unit 3 explains recreation and leisure time skills which are very important in social skills development.

How to Train?

- Give chances to learn the skills through regular selected activities.
- Gradually reduce the number of repeated instructions and observe his performance in natural environments.
- Include him as a family member, in all family get together.
- Give him chances to participate in social and religious functions. Outings help in enhancing social skill training.
- Accept the mentally retarded child as a member of the family and the community.

1. *Waits for Need to be Fulfilled*

1. List out some activities, which provide chances to train the child to wait for his needs to be fulfilled.
2. Initially simulate situations to make him wait for needs to be fulfilled for a shorter period of time.
3. Gradually increase the time of waiting in the simulated/ actual situation.

Finally, train him to wait in an actual situation: play time, meal time, conversation, shopping...........

While doing so, explain to him in a friendly manner that you are busy doing something and that you would attend to his needs shortly. Make sure that he understands. When you go to attend to him appreciate him for having waited. This would strengthen the child's behaviour and it is likely that he would accept the situation and wait when the need arises again.

List of Activities

- *Play-time:* Waits for the swing while another child is swinging on it.
- *Meal-time:* Waits for the food to be served, when mother is busy.
- *Conversation:* Waits for his turn to talk in a group situation.
- Knocks at the door and waits for the response.
- *Shopping situation:* Waits till the shop-keeper settles the accounts with a customer who is ahead.

2. ***Plays with Peer Sharing Objects***

1. List out activities where the child has to share.
2. *Play- time:* When the child plays with a ball, let another child join him to share and play with the ball after requesting him.
3. When he plays with toys like blocks and beads let other children also share and play with him, after requesting the child.
4. *Meal- time:* Give him opportunities to share food/snacks with other family members and friends.

Sharing of Personal Items

- In case, siblings and peers need objects from him (pencil, eraser...) guide him to help giving objects and get them back after use.
- When friends and relatives come to his house, create situations so that the child can share his objects.
- Create situations where he requests other children for sharing their objects, as well as, he is requested by others for which he obliges.

3. *Greets Others*

- At home.
- Give the child chances to see when family members great others. Let the child also join them.
- Introduce the words, which are used for greetings, Namaste, Vanakkam, good morning, good afternoon and good evening.
- Also introduce the appropriate bodily gestures that would go with the greeting.

At School

- If the child goes to school, train him to greet his friends when he meets them.
- Take him to the teacher, and demonstrate how to great him/her when the child meets him/her, first in the morning.
- Train him to greet other teachers and elders in the school.
- Generally children learn to greet in the school because they observe all the other children doing so and they tend to imitate others. Provide opportunity for observing and imitating.

In the Community

- When you take the child for outing, let him observe, how you greet others. Take time to train him also to greet the elders and friends he meets on the way.
- When he visits friends and relatives, train him how to wish them, when he enters their home.
- If he forgets, you wish first so that he would remember to do so. Giving such clues is better than scolding the child for not doing an activity.

4. ***Obeys Commands***

- As the child learns to follow instructions train him to obey his family members. Initially select simple commands which the child likes to do (to call someone, to play with a toy, to bring something which he likes,.....). Appreciate him immediately when he obeys.
- As he learns to attend to his personal needs such as brushing, toileting, bathing, dressing and grooming, give commands related to his daily routine so that he will develop the habit of doing it on time.
- As a next step, give him instructions related to household activities. If he has problems in understanding, demonstrate and ask him to do by watching you. Initially appreciate him for his near correct attempts.
- Gradually start giving commands related to proper social behaviour. For example, if he unnecessarily shouts/runs/smiles, tell him to stop. If he does not obey, ignore him, but do not yield to his demands. When he is ignored, make sure that he does not have any objects around him that would hurt him. If consistently followed, this would help in developing obedience in the child.

5. ***Says 'Please', 'Thank You' and 'Sorry'***

As the child starts to follow instructions and communicate needs, it is time to use the words 'Please', 'Thank you' and 'Sorry'. These three words are called 'the magic words' as they lead to instant acceptance by others.

Says 'Please'

- Use the word 'Please' when you ask the child or someone to do a favour. For example, 'Please, bring that plate', 'Please cut the vegetables', 'Please wait for a minute' and so on.
- Give him chances to use the word 'Please'. If he does not speak let him gesture the expression. Whenever, he asks for a favour, insist, on his saying or gesturing 'please' before you fulfill it.

Says 'Thank you'

Let the child observe and listen when you use the word 'Thank you'. Create situations for the child to use 'Thank you' or gesture the expression whenever, he receives objects or help from others.

Says 'Sorry'

The concept of 'Sorry' can be taught only when the child is able to understand that he has done something wrong. Explain and train him to use the word 'sorry' when he misbehaves or forgets to do what he was told to do or when he hurts others unintentionally or intentionally.

Appreciate him when he uses the words 'Please', 'Thank you', and 'Sorry' appropriately. When the child forgets to use the word remind him by saying 'Where's the magic word?'

6. *Helps Parents in Household Tasks*

- In the initial stage, let the child watch when the family members are involved in different household tasks. Motivate him to join you. Appreciate his willingness and attempts.
- Depending on the age and ability level of the child list out some household activities in which he can help the family members: bringing water, helping to wash, drying and arranging utensils, helping to arrange clothes in an almirah, cleaning vegetables, watering plants, making beds and so on. Let his involvement be minimal and in easy tasks in the beginning. Appreciate him for his assistance. Gradually increase the duration and difficulty of task.
- As he learns, list a few activities in which he can regularly help the family members. Make sure that you do not choose activities beyond his capabilities or too easy and boring.

- Appreciate and reward his attempts and success.
- Highlight his help when all family members are present.
- This will motivate him to help you further.

7. *Asks Permission*

At Home

- Show the child his belongings at home: clothes, books, bag, tooth brush, slippers and so on. Explain to him those are His/Her belongings.
- Similarly, show the belonging of others and tell him/her that they belong to so and so.
- If he wants to use anything, which is not his, tell him that he should ask permission from the respective persons.
- When you use the belongings of others including the child's ask for permission and allow the child to watch. Let all the family members follow this so that the child is more likely to do so and thus learn to ask for permission. Is it not a good habit for us also?

At School

If the child attends school, give him chances to ask permission. For example, in case he wants to borrow a toy/a pencil/a book, let him ask politely for permission and use the words 'please' and 'thank you' appropriately.

In the Community

When the child visits friends and relatives, make sure that he does not take anything without permission. Encourage him to ask permission to take a toy to play, to see an album and so on. Explain to the friends and relatives that he is being trained in asking for permission so that they also cooperate and assist in the training.

8. *Takes Turn*

List out occasions where he has to take his turn.

At Home

Assign duties to the family members. Let him to do the work when his turn comes, waiting for bathroom to be vacant for bathing, waiting to use the wash basin or washing area for brushing and so on.

At School

- To get into the school van, expose him to the queue system and let him wait to take his turn.
- Assign duties to the children – cleaning, arranging, taking messages and so on. Explain when his turn comes and how to perform his duty.
- Waiting for his turn at lunch – time, in singing song, in group game situations and other such activities must be encouraged.

In the Community

- At a bus stand, where he has to stand in queue to get the ticket and get into the bus, provide actual experience.
- In a public milk booth, show how people wait and take their turns. Give him chances.
- Take him with you to banks, railway stations, cinema theatres and such other areas where waiting for one's turn is necessary.

9. *Participates Appropriately at Meal Time*

Setting Table

- Take the child's help to set the table and/or arrange dishes as per the family customs.
- Depending on the number of family members tell him to get enough plates and tumblers. Tell him to get food items like water, curd and pickles, which are not hot, from kitchen and keep on the table/ dining area. Initially physically assist him so that he does not drop them down.

Serving in a Family Setting

- Let the child also sit in proper place with the other family members.
- Train him to serve food for himself and others without spilling. Initially let him start with items like papad, which will not spill. Gradually move to solid food items and finally liquid and sticky items.
- Demonstrate how to request for food if he wants.

Taking Part in Clearing and Cleaning

- Tell the child to wait for everybody to finish to get-up/leave the table.
- Make sure he washes his hands and mouth properly.
- Give him chances to clear the table/dining place.
- Encourage the child to clean the utensils and keep in proper place.

Give chances and check whether he follows appropriate manners when you take him to restaurants and social functions. Appreciate his appropriate responses.

Training in this should be based on his comprehension and physical ability. Give chances to participate in a number of activities, based on his ability level.

10. Dresses and Grooms Appropriately to the Situations

Appropriate dressing and grooming skills are necessary for social acceptance. It is essential that one knows to differentiate and use clothings appropriate to the situation.

At Home

Provide the child a place in the almirah to keep separately the clothe's which he has to wear at home during different household/play activities.

At School

If he has too wear the uniform when he goes to school, tell him the need and keep it for that purpose. As soon as he comes home remind him to change from the uniform to home clothes. Depending on his age and ability, he can be taught to maintain his clothings.

Various Functions

Most of the households have the clothing for occasions stored safely in one place. Give the child also a place there to keep his clothings. Explain to him that they are expensive clothes, not easily washable and hence must be maintained carefully when worn and also when stored. Allow him to participate in storing them carefully.

Various Seasons

Discuss about the different seasons in a year. Show him in pictures and TV. Explain the need to wear warm clothes in winter and light clothes in summer. Train him to wear the different clothes and maintain them.

11. *Visits and Invites Relatives and Friends*

Visits Relatives and Friends

Do not hesitate to take the child when the family members visit relatives and friends. Give him chances to wish them appropriately, use polite language, use words like 'please' and 'thank you' when needed, and exhibit good manners.

Depending on the child's level of functioning and the distance of the relative's house train him to go and come back by himself.

Invites Relatives and Friends

When the child visits the relatives and friends, let him see when you invite them to your house. Give him chances to invite his friends/relatives to his home, after getting his parents permission to do so.

Explain to him how to receive them when they come, talk to them, play with them and eat with them. Be with the child, model the activities so that he can follow. Gradually, reduce the help, and guide him to receive his friends and relatives.

Do not be ashamed of introducing the child to others. He is a member of your family and he deserves to participate in the family gathering.

12. *Participates in Parties*

At Home

During functions at home include the child as a family member. Let him participate in arrangements and reception of guests. Give him chances to sit with the family members and guests during parties.

At School

Usually in schools, the teachers organize functions and give specific responsibilities to each child with intimation to parents. Cooperate with the teachers in helping the child to effectively participate in the part or function.

In the Community

As he learns to take part in parties at home and school give him chances to go for the social functions. Till he becomes independent to take part with his friends, take him with you and train him in good manners which he has to observe. The more chances we give, the better competence the child gains.

Appreciate and reward him for his appropriate behaviour.

13. *Behaves Appropriately with Opposite Sex*

At Home

As the child grows, it is important to train him to behave appropriately with the opposite sex. Check and train him for proper behaviour with the brothers/sisters at home. The acceptable interaction between boys and girls vary from culture to culture. Train suitably.

When friends/relatives visit your home, if the trainee is a boy, train him to receive and wish a girl and vice versa.

Instead of keeping him/her away from the persons in the opposite sex, expose him to such situations under supervision so that he develops acceptable manners. Show that a physical distance is maintained when one interacts with persons of the other sex.

Community

Take the child also for outings and functions. Give him chances to talk to boys and girls of his age group. Supervise and help when needed, during their interaction. Explain the do's and don'ts then and there so that he does not commit the same error again.

14. *Returns Borrowed Materials*

1. In the initial stage, create situations so that the child can ask for things. Tell him to return it after use. If he returns reward him, if he forgets to return, remind him. Have more chances to learn the skill of returning borrowed things. You may borrow things from him and return to him. Remember to thank him. He is likely to follow your foot- steps.

2. Insist that borrowed materials must be used very carefully so that they do not get damaged. They should be returned to the lender as soon as the need is fulfilled.
3. Explain to him that in case he needs an article from anther person—a pencil, a scissor, an umbrella, or a book—he should ask politely and return it on time.

Do not forget to tell the child that as far as possible we use our own things rather than borrowed ones !!

15. *Identifies Human Service Persons and Community Helpers*

Let him watch the services of person who deliver newspaper, milk, gas and such other things.

Provide opportunity to him to know about other community helpers such as police- man, postman, doctor, people from electricity board, station master and others whom we come in contact with once in a while. Take him with you, when you meet these people and take time to explain to the child the role of these people in making our life easier. If possible let them talk to him about their work. Show him important people and events in the newspaper and television.

(The Unit 2, continues with social skills training. Unit 3, explains the leisure-time and recreational activities which would help to improve social skills in persons with mental retardation.)

Unit Summary

Intensive training is needed to cultivate appropriate social behaviours in the persons with Mental Retardation. The training should started early in life.

The family, the relatives, neighbours, friends and the society at large are responsible for the social skills training of the persons with mental retardation.

The persons with mental retardation need stimulation, repeated chances, supervision and training to develop proper skills.

Check Your Progress

- Explain the need and importance of social skills training for persons with mental retardation.

- Mention 5 social skills, which are to be taught at primary and secondary levels.
- Explain the method to be teach to identify human service persons and community helpers.

Assignment/Activities

Prepare a small skit to teach social skills. Select the children and practice to perform the skit during a function.

Points for Discussion/Clarification

....

....

....

....

REFERENCE

Narayan, J. and Thressiakutty, A.T. (2001), *Social Skills, Package for Trainers*, NIMH, Secunderabad.

UNIT–5

Teaching Social Skills for Varied Situations Including When in Distress/Exploited

STRUCTURE

- Introduction
- Objectives
- Personal – Social Skills
- Developing Social Relationship of the Persons with M.R.
- Unit Summary
- Check Your Progress
- Assignment/ Activities
- Points for Clarification/ Discussion
- Reference

5

Teaching Social Skills for Varied Situations Including When in Distress/Exploited

Introduction

Concepts of self, other and their interactions include the elements of risk and trust in classroom activities. Risk is one element in the process of problem-solving, while trust is essential to self-respect. Risk can be defined by such social factors as self-esteem, popularity with peers, and even teacher approval. The teacher should identify the factors and objectives that contribute to the student's self-awareness and his relationship with others.

Objectives

After going through this unit the trainees will be able to

- identify personal-social skills to be taught to the adolescent and adults with mental retardation.
- develop teach the personal-social skills with suitable activities in different situations.

Personal – Social Skills

1. *Achieving Self-Awareness*

Legislation guarantees the people with disabilities equal rights for education, transportation and employment. They are entering the main stream of society. At the same time society tries to keep them away with restrictions. The achievement of self-awareness has so much to do with bearing a contributing and productive member of society.

2. *Attaining Sense of Body*

Every maturational change requires a modification in the individual's concept of the body. This process includes a changing image of the self. A positive body image contributes to the individual's sense of ability and worth. Teachers, parents and therapists help the individual develop a positive body image by providing adequate information related to the parts of the body, their functions and the person's physical characteristics.

Each stage of development requires different kinds and amounts of information. Children at 7 years of age will not ask of the same question as adolescent or adults at 40 years of age. Thus needs very and the answers must match the unique physical characteristics of the individuals.

3. *Identifying Interests and Abilities*

Teachers should plan activities that require students to identify interest, list personal abilities and plan strategies to implement selected goals.

4. *Identifying Emotions*

Teachers can begin classroom activities that deal with emotions. Primary level students should identify the emotions such as happiness, sadness and anger. They should be trained to express the emotions in an appropriate way. Older children should begin to learn how to recognize various emotions expressed in different ways, for example body language facial expressions and tone of voice.

Another major objective in this area is to develop an ability to distinguish the consequences of emotions, For example, an expression of anger by an employer may have different consequences than a similar demonstration by an employee.

Activity

Cut pictures from newspaper and have a discussion on emotions expressed in various ways. Prepare a skit in which the students contact and express the emotions.

5. *Identifying Needs*

Irrespective of the disabilities, the students have physical, psychological and social needs like any other normal persons. Let the students identify their needs and have a discussion on the needs and the ways to meet the needs.

6. *Understanding the Physical Self*

Understanding the physical self-contains objectives that are specific to the sexual role of the individuals. The activities should enable students to develop an awareness of the similarities and differences in the anatomy and functioning of the male and female.

7. *Acquiring Self-Confidence*

In some instances people with disabilities were not even regarded as human beings but as the embodiment of evil sprits. Despite these opinions and attitudes, the individuals must build a concept of himself as a capable human being so that he can reach personal objective in life.

8. *Expressing Feeling of Worth*

Teachers and parents should provide opportunities in which students express how they feel about themselves in relationship to their accomplishments, successes and failures. What experiences cause students to feel good, worthy or pleased with their accomplishments? What experiences frustrate them?

9. *Telling How Others See Him*

What others think of us influences our attitude towards the self. These attitudes are used as a basis for further judgements. Parents and teachers cannot control the attitudes of the other people, in some cases. But the students can be taught to observe another person's responses that reflect either positive or negative attitude. The lessons should emphasis positive reactions that reflect the handicapped individual's self-respect.

10. *Accepting Praise*

The students need experiences in which others confirm and show respect for their behaviour. Experiences include daily activities at home, school and other environments, which the students are contributing members of the society.

11. *Accepting Criticism*

The teacher can train the students to accept criticism by providing as much respect for the students while his work being analyzed. Respect with criticism builds self- confidence. An attitude of respect says to the student," you are someone". The critical element conveys the message, "you are someone who can improve on this mistake." The improvement reinforces the previous steps in process.

12. *Achieving Socially Responsible Behaviour*

Some of the positive traits are cooperation, cheerfulness and dependability necessary in employment situations. For students who experience problems in performing acceptable behaviour, the teacher may structure a system in which there is a conscious effort to modify the behaviour toward the set objectives.

13. *Demonstrating Proper Behaviour in Public Places*

The student should be able to identify behaviours that are appropriate and expected of him in such places as restaurant, transportation, recreational settings and public meetings. These behaviours are learned from the family and peer group. If it is necessary for the teacher to modify these behaviours, the student, teacher and family members should work together to achieve the goal.

14. *Developing Respect for the Rights and Properties of Others*

The students should be able to differentiate what belongs to them from what belongs to someone else. These basic lessons can be initiated at class level. The rights of others become more complicated as individuals grow older especially regarding the family properties and public properties.

15. *Recognizing Personal Roles*

Students should be able to describe and demonstrate responsible behaviour to individuals identified with a specific role (employer, parent and child) as well as groups. Parents should involve their children in as many family activities and decisions as possible.

16. *Achieving Problem-Solving Skills*

The process of problem-solving is intrinsic to education Reading, writing, calculating and other basic skills prepare students to make appropriate decisions.

17. *Differentiating Bipolar Concepts*

Good and evil, positive and negative are few terms often used in reference to issues and relationships. But problems and to issues and relationships. But problems and relationships do not fall into such a neat dichotomy. There may be several solutions to a problem or positions on an issue creating several situations of daily living.

18. *Looking at Alternatives*

Exercises related to differentiation if he/she accepts, expose him/her to the possibility that other solutions or positions can be used to solve problem, and that the person must search for alternatives. A simple example the student is late for his class/work. How can he reach on time? Can he take the help from someone to guide him? Should he go by walk/bus/auto?

The student has a doubt which medicine he should take? How can he solve the problem?

The student has three job opportunities, what criteria he would use to select the proper one?

19. *Anticipating Consequences*

Anticipating the consequences of a decision is the most difficult component to examine in the problem-solving process. Everyday decisions are experienced by all of us and their consequences can be used as guides for teaching this respect.

20. *Aware of Where to Find Good Advice*

The students should be taught to identify the resources in their communities that can provide assistance in personal and family decision-making.

Developing Social Relationship of the Persons with M.R.

Children with mental retardation like the normal children have the capacity to grow and develop within the limits. But they need an environment conducive to growth and development. The process and means of growth and development depend on the degree of their retardation, psychological and emotional capacities and the environment in which they live in. There growth and development may be facilitated in a therapeutic environment providing opportunity for functional programmes, which usually emphasis social skills with collaboration of parents, teachers, peers, relatives and the psychiatric social worker.

The mentally retarded children undergo the same maturation process as other children do, excepting some late milestone. However, the difference between the pattern of social relations and social maturity of the mentally retarded and the normal is quite obvious. The socio grams of the retarded children, if drawn, will show a low range of social relationship since their interaction are confined to limited persons in these environments and their social functioning, interpersonal relationship and role performance present the evidences that the persons with mental retardation are not socially so matured as the normal.

1. *Outing*

The children of late-latency age show more inclination in getting themselves involved in activities requiring contact with outside social world. The want to widen their social contacts and outings, it is one of the most important function through which they extend their social contacts.

2. *Participation in Family Responsibilities*

The sense of belonging to the family is one of the most important criterion to measure the social maturity of the children. The children are taught to participate in different household activities and share responsibilities with the family. The children experience growth and development through a shared responsibility with family and through it experience acceptance, recognition and belongings.

3. *Schooling*

Schooling is itself a stressful situation for the pre-latency children because they have to remain departed from their parents and homes. Therefore, they need an atmosphere of security, confidence and trust.

Their contracts with the teachers, class-mates and other school children expand their social contact and functioning. Hence, a healthy environment in school programmes and preparation for schooling will be helpful to them. The personality of these children is modified by their contact with the school. Their personal relations expand to include persons in the school and neighbourhood. During this period they acquire a larger vocabulary, begin to read and to hear about the people who lived before him and how they behaved and mould their school behaviour.

4. *Participation in Class Programmes*

A classroom atmosphere of competence and trust is an essential condition favourable of social development. Class situations and programmes, if arranged keeping in view of the family situation, foundation of personality in childhood, emotional life, social life, religious life and behaviour patterns will be helpful for a healthy participation of the children in the class. The conditions of acceptance, confidence and trust will be the result.

5. *Meeting with Other Retarded Children*

The children seek a friendly atmosphere and need companion's support acceptance and encouragements. Emotional relationship with their peer group and the efforts in establishing themselves successfully in-group are of utmost importance. The way they meet with other children, interact with them, and involve them in the activities of the peer group show their social growth and development. Their ego ideal, their sense of values and their social contacts had their roots in such societal experiences.

6. *Participation In-group Activities*

During pre-adolescent years team spirit, class spirits, group spirits and group loyalties develop. The school child, normal or, retarded, needs a variety of stimulating experiences and these experiences, his personal needs, desires and interest are fulfilled through participation in group activities. The child accepts the group goals, assumes responsibilities, shares with group members, accepts the limitations of the group, participates in activities and thereby immediate and/or sustained gratification of the needs and interests of the child is attended.

The mentally retarded children are observed in therapeutically organized groups by the psychiatric social workers and in free groups where the children and free to participate in any activity which they themselves decide. In free groups, they may also choose with whom they would participate and with whom they would not.

Unit Summary

Children with mental retardation, like the normal children, have the capacity to grow and develop within their limits. But they need an environment conducive to growth and development.

The teachers should identify the factors and objectives that contribute to the student's self-awareness and his relationship with others. The important personal and social skills are:

- Achieving self-awareness
- Attaining sense of body
- Identifying interests and abilities
- Identifying emotions
- Identifying needs
- Understanding the physical self
- Acquiring self-confidence
- Expressing feeling of work
- Telling how others see him
- Accepting praise
- Accepting criticism
- Achieving socially responsible behaviour
- Demonstrating proper behaviour in public places
- Developing respect for the rights and properties of others
- Recognizing personal roles
- Achieving problem-solving skills
- Differentiating bipolar concepts
- Looking at alternatives
- Anticipating consequence
- Aware of where to find good advice.

The social skills can be nurtured through outings, participating in family responsibilities, participation in class programmes, meeting with other special children and engaging in group activities.

Check Your Progress

- Explain 10 higher-level personal and social skills, which can be taught to the persons with mental retardation attending pre-vocational level.
- Discuss the method to teach the children with mental retardation to identify the emotions and express them in an appropriate way.
- How can social skills be nurtured in persons with mental retardation?
- Briefly discuss how would you teach the following:
  1. Attaining sense of body.
  2. Expressing feelings of worth.
  3. Achieving problem-solving skills.

Assignment/Activities

Prepare a poster/captions on the need of social skills training for persons with mental retardation.

Points for Discussion/Clarification

....

....

....

....

REFERENCE

Kokasa, C. (1985), *Career Education for Handicapped Individuals* (IInd Edition). Lond: Chares, E. Merril.

UNIT–6

Recreation and Leisure Need–Age Appropriate Activities–Individuals and Group Situations for Persons with Mental Retardation

STRUCTURE

- Introduction
- Objectives
- Definition
- Characteristics of Leisure Programmes
- Importance of Leisure Programmes
- Leisure in the Home Community
- Identifying and Selecting Skills for Instruction
- Types of Leisure and Recreational Activities
- Definition of Types of Leisure
- Yoga
- Breathing Techniques
- Leisure Skills and Socialization
- Role of Special Olympics
- Types of Sports
- Training of Coaches
- Volunteers
- Very Special Arts
- Abilympics
- National Festival of Music and Dance
- Developing a Well- balanced Recreation Programme
- Adaptation Strategies

- Hobbies
- Unit Summary
- Check Your Progress
- Assignment/Activities
- Points for Discussion/Clarification
- Reference

6

Recreation and Leisure Need–Age Appropriate Activities–Individuals and Group Situations for Persons with Mental Retardation

Introduction

Formal programming may be needed to provide people with mental retardation with an adequate repertoire of leisure skills. Usually people with mental retardation after their school hours/ working hours, spend their time watching a little television, going out for a cup of coffee, and going to bed early. A wider repertoire of leisure activities helps them to use their leisure time more useful and enjoyable.

Objectives

After going through this unit the trainees will able to

- define the term leisure.
- describe characteristics and importance of leisure and recreational programmes.
- identify and trained persons with mental retardation in leisure time activities.

Definition

The word 'leisure' is derived from Latin word "Licere" meaning to be free. This definition suggests not only that leisure time is free time, but also that leisure activities must be freely chosen if they are to satisfy an individual's personal and social needs. For adults with mental retardation, free choice is often restricted. Restrictions may stem from a restrictive living arrangement, limited access to community recreation opportunities and skills limitations.

Characteristics of Leisure Programmes

Four elements that should characterize recreational and leisure programme are:

(a) Fun and enjoyment.
(b) Constructive or purposeful behaviour.
(c) Participation.
(d) Self-initiated behaviour and choice.

(a) Fun and Enjoyment

This element is perhaps the most differentiating characteristic between leisure and other major skills domain such as work, domestic/home/living and community functioning. Certainly in implementing leisure programme the teacher must be sensitive in providing an enjoyable and fun atmosphere for students with activities, which are naturally reinforcing. Teaching students to label boxes and stitch buttons are not considered "fun".

(b) Constructive or Purposeful Behaviour Nurture

Imagine a severely retarded woman who rocks her body constantly sitting in her room, smiling and laughing at all the time. Of course, this is not the type of leisure which is normalizing and which service providers want to encourage.

(c) Participation

Leisure is one co-curricular area in Special Education. If one can enjoy an activity by limited involvement, the leisure goals will be met. The strategies to improve participation through adaptation are discussed in this unit.

(d) Self-initiated Behaviour and Choice

The persons with severe handicaps may not demonstrate self-initiated responses. Leisure is more of a choice activity than any other skill domain. The educators and care-takers should be sensitive to this component.

To sum up, the ultimate result, if an appropriate leisure programme, should allow the person to initiate activities, which are enjoyable to him/her.

There should be a repertoire of activities that can be taught and subsequently for which the materials are made available.

Rote and mechanical use of one object for months and months is not the ultimate objective of a well-designed leisure programme.

Importance of Leisure Programmes

Leisure programmes need to be formalized and structured for all level of persons with mental retardation. This requires systematic instruction. The individual education plans should reflect leisure objectives for acquisition and generalization. Some of the reasons for emphasizing leisure programme are:

(a) Enhancing Quality Life

Persons with mental retardation have a large amount of free time available. Imposed leisure time activities and capabilities can have a positive effect on their quality of life. With severely multiple and non-ambulatory profoundly retarded individuals, the amount of free time is extensive. It is necessary that we study ways in which to expand the leisure and recreational opportunities for these individuals.

(b) Prevention of Institutionalization

Developing appropriate leisure programmes can facilitate community retention of severely mentally retarded individuals. It is apparent that parent, family members and care-takers will be more willing to maintain a child at home who can play independently and not exhibit destructive behaviour.

(c) Community and Vocational Adjustment

Competence in social, leisure and other community skills is crucial in helping persons with mental retardation adjust in the community and become fully integrated.

(d) Behaviour Management

The common characteristic of individuals with mental retardation especially severe retardation is behaviour problems, which can lead to serious management problems. Numerous investigators have found that leisure skills training is an excellent means of reducing the behavioural problems. Inappropriate social behaviours can be reduced through constructive leisure time activities.

The above reasons only briefly touch on the value of leisure instruction. Hopefully, the educators can visualize the benefits of a well-planned recreation programme.

Leisure in the Home Community

Most leisure programmes occurred in school classroom or institutional environment. There is a need to give more attention for community based leisure instruction.

A leisure skill area, which is consistently practiced, should occur most frequently either at home or in a community setting.

Many more home training programmes and efforts at generalization of leisure skills must be initiated.

The trainers should be aware of the need of practicing in natural environments in which they are supposed to occur.

Identifying and Selecting Skills for Instruction

There are several factors, which need to be considered.

(a) Chronological Age-appropriations

Selection of age appropriate activities is necessary to communicate the competence and dignity of persons with mental retardation.

(b) Attitude of Parents and Family Members

A second factor in selecting leisure skills relates to the attitude of parents and other family members and the availability of leisure materials in the home environment. Without sensitivity to this issue, the carry over of this leisure programmes into the home will be greatly limited. The type of community resources in a given locality is also essential while deciding the leisure skills for instruction.

(c) Attitude, Aptitude and Skills of the Clients

The attitude, aptitude and the ability to learn the skills are also crucial when identifying the leisure time skills. The children also should be given freedom to select the activities of their choice.

The Table 1 (leisure activity selection checklist) have divided skill selection into major categories of normalization philosophy, individualization and environment.

Table–1 : Leisure Activity Selection Checklist

Sl. No.	*Normalization*	*Yes/No*
1.	Age appropriateness	
2.	Attraction	
3.	Environmental Flexibility	
4.	Degree of supervision	
5.	Longitudinal application	
Sl. No.	*Normalization*	*Yes/No*
1.	Skill level flexibility	
2.	Prosthetic Capabilities	
3.	Re-enforcement power	
Sl. No.	*Normalization*	*Yes/No*
1.	Availability	
2.	Desirability	
3.	Safety	
4.	Space Conception	
5.	Expenses	

Types of Leisure and Recreational Activities

Leisure and recreational activities have been categorized in variety of ways, which include:

- Physical activities
- Cultural activities
- Social activities
- Mental activities
- Outdoor and indoor activities
- Spectator and participant activities
- Passive and active activities
- Co-operative and competent activities
- Community- based activities
- Sports and games
- Hobbies and toy play.

The above-mentioned activities have been classified in this unit into sports, games, hobbies and toy play because these four categories encompass all types of functional and community-based activities. Within each category, both indoor and outdoor, independent and cooperative activities are given in the following pages with examples of activities from each category that have been successfully instructed to persons with mental retardation.

Definition of Types of Leisure

(a) Object Manipulation

Appropriate manipulation of leisure materials is the basis of toy play. The manipulation skills are the pre-requisites to participate in sports, games and hobbies.

Object manipulation skills can be taught simultaneously as separate leisure objectives, example: catching ball and within the context of more leisure activities, example, playing a modified soft ball. The younger child and the very unskilled student should have a greater emphasis on specific object manipulation skills in his/her leisure skills curriculum.

Table–2 : Toy Play/ Manipulation

Balls	Dolls	Hammer toys	Musical toys
Block	Frisbee	Tricycle	Puppets
Crayon		Sewing material	Rocking toys
Trucks/Plains			
Moving toy		Record player	Pick-up games
Marbles		Telephone	

Appropriate only for younger students.

(b) Sports

Sports are organized activities involving some type of rules, complex gross and fine motor movements and the exertion of physical energy. Some sports involve single participant while others involve two or more.

Sports are important part of our culture because of their relationship with health and fitness and because much of our leisure time is spent as sports spectators. Some of the sports skills that can successfully be taught persons with mental retardation include:

- Individual exercises.
- Use of playground exercises.
- Swimming.
- Weight training.
- Jogging.

Although sports typically involve a number of very complex motor pattern and intricate rules, most severely handicapped persons can at least be taught to practically participate in some community-based sports. In many cases, some kind of adaptation will have to be made. The instructor must analysis the sport in terms of the motor pattern involved, the separate skill sequences comprising the activity and the adaptations possible. Some sports are so difficult to learn those, which involve at least complicated motor patterns and rules, but are still age-appropriate should be instructed first.

For example, volleyball is a simpler team sport than softball or basketball because it entails only striking, jumping, sliding and running and has fewer rules. Examples of sports that may be taught to persons with mental retardation are given in the table.

Sports/Fitness Activities

↓

Independent or Individual Activities

↓

Yoga	Biking	Dancing
Walking	Weight training	Jogging
Swimming	Wrong playground equipment	
Skating	Jumping rope	

Dual/Cooperative Activities

Boating	Hand ball	
Bowling	Frisbee	Gymnastics
Dancing		

(*a*) Team Sports

Hockey	Basket ball	Kabbady
Softball	Volley ball	Floor Hockey
Cricket		

(c) Games

Like sports, games usually involve some sort of rules. However, games one typically played purely for enjoyment and they are really leisure activities. Games can be physical, involving complex gross motor pattern or more passive, less open-ended or structured like checkers and certain card games.

Two of major considerations in teaching games are making sure that the activities and materials chosen are chronologically age-appropriate and provide opportunities for participants to interact and share with each other. Examples are given below:

Sample Games Appropriate for Persons Utilized

Checkers	Caroms
Picture	Musical chair
Video games	Simon songs
Yard games	Marble game
Ping pong	

(d) Hobbies

The aim of hobby participation is enjoyment. A hobby is any recreational activity in which one can participate continuously, sometimes life long basis. It may be an activity in which one physically participates or an event in which the participant becomes a spectator (example: watching movie, sports, listening music).

Very often persons with mental retardation especially moderate and severe categories do not have hobbies because they have never been taught to participate in certain activities purely for enjoyment over an extended period of time. For a person to really have a hobby, he/she initially should be taught a variety of activities and then be allowed to choose the ones that are most enjoyable.

Hobbies can be sports, games, cooking, painting, observing and listening. Examples are given on next page.

Yoga

Yoga is a system of mental, spiritual and physical development, which originated in our country. Yoga means to bind together. There

Hobbies

Pet care	Cooking	Books and magazines
Plant care	.	Collecting
Needle work	Wood work	Movies
Painting	Weaving	
Music	Sports watching	Cultural activities

are many branches of Yoga. The popularly used one is *Hatha* Yoga, which involves expression and conservation of energy. This type of yoga incorporates asanas (postures) along with *pranayama* (breathing exercises). Yoga is being tried quite effectively to control children with hyperactivity.

The teacher must be well-trained in yoga before teaching children with mental retardation.

Differences Between Physical Exercise and Yoga

- Yoga is exercise without visible movement. Exercises emphasize movement.
- Exercise usually involves a number of several bounces/ stretches/stretches in a given time. Yoga stresses on a single slow contraction of certain muscles followed by relaxation.
- Exercise usually entails some pain and discomfort. In Yoga, the number of repetitions is not increased. The duration of time in which each Asana is held increases in accordance with ease of performance.
- Exercises stress the development of strength – flexibility and endurance. Yoga stresses relaxation, balance, self-control.

Practice of Yoga is being tried with children with mental retardation to

- improve their general health.
- increase attention span.
- improve social and communication skills.
- reduce hyperactivity.
- control seizures.

Yoga as a form of physical exercise is being used in special schools for the mentally retarded children to develop gross and fine motor skills and to improve general health.

Practice of Yoga involves *Asana*–meaning posture and *Pranayama*—meaning regulated breathing. An individual doing *Asana* must experience comfort and should maintain steadiness in given posture (Desikachar, 1982).

Pranayama is usually practiced in a comfortable sitting position. It involves breathing in holding breath, exhalation and retention after exhalation.

There are five basic positions in which Asanas can be performed. 1. Standing, 2. Supine (lying), 3. Inverted, 4. Prone (lying) and 5. Sitting, kneeling.

Breathing Techniques

- Initially demonstrate and provide physical and verbal prompts.
- Do not limit instructions to verbal level only. Repeat many times to help him achieve steadiness in given posture.
- Do not introduce breathing technique in the beginning. Allow students to practice simple *asanas* regularly, breathing as usual. Once they are comfortable with movement and posture, introduce breathing. Many are excellent mimics, so demonstrate breathing clearly.
- Start with exhalation. Some children may not comprehend when you say 'breathe out'. So try making them say 'aah' or 'ha' which makes them automatically exhale, including use of abdomen. Once they exhale, inhalation naturally follows.
- To motivate inhalation, sprinkle perfume on their hand and ask them to smell it.
- Some children may comprehend breathing in, retention and exhaling to count, such as 1,2,3,4 but many may not. Some may know just 1 and 2. In such cases, say one and two in a slow manner, stretching the word as you say. Say stop – and indicate with raised palm when you want them to retain breath. Again say one..... two.... slowly to release. Repeating the word one slowly also provides an excellent opportunity to inhale, retain and exhale breath.
- To teach exhalation to children with associated visual and hearing impairments: For a child with visual impairment, hold his hand in front of your mouth when you exhale. Ask

him to imitate. For a hearing impaired child-breathe in front of a mirror and let him observe what happens.

Leisure Skills and Socialization

Independent, cooperative and competitive social contexts can exist for many of the four types of leisure described in the earlier section. What will be presented next is a brief review of each of these social situations, their relative importance, and related programme development information relevant to each.

(a) Independent Leisure

Independent or isolative leisure usually refers to an individual interacting with an object or engaging in an activity alone. This situation suggests that this person is able to exhibit leisure for a sustained period with minimal adult supervision. The first stage in the development of independent leisure activities is learning to complete one or more simple leisure activities independently.

Value of Independent Leisure

The ability to interact with objects constructively and for a sustained period of time eases tension on the part of the family numbers, eases the search for baby sitters, and usually enhances the acceptance of the child in the home and community. In addition, it should also be noted that many students would have no peers to play with, after school. Hence, independent leisure will be the only social context available.

There are other reasons for promoting independent play. These relate to the student's feeling better about himself/herself because of competence in initiating leisure skills, the likelihood of reduced behaviour management problems and the facility with which other important collateral skills such as communication and motor skills may be trained. A comprehensive leisure education programme is complete only if it contains instruction for the development of independent leisure skills.

(b) Basic Principle Involved in Developing Independent Leisure Physical Proximity Approach

If an individual refuses to interact with objects, the instructor can place the materials physically closer to the individuals.

(c) Modeling

These techniques have been an essential component of most play and leisure skill training programmes for the children with severe mental retardation.

Verbal Instructions

Verbal instructions can be made use in playground equipment related play activities.

Physical Prompting and Chaining

These strategies can be used especially in the initial stages of training individuals who are either very poor verbal control or who have had no previous instruction in leisure skills.

The danger with physical guidance is that when this form of help is extended over a time, it may become difficult to withdraw teacher assistance and allow for more independent behaviours. The use of task analysis for leisure instruction is greatly enhanced.

(d) Cooperative Leisure

The ability to participate jointly in an activity with a peer in a group is a developmentally more advanced level of socialization.

Value of Cooperative Leisure

- Cooperative leisure facilitates friendships.
- When non-disabled people are paired with disabled peers, the severely disabled students may be perceived in a more normal light.
- Cooperative leisure usually requires taking turn, sharing, and waiting for others. These are very important skills, which are essential for acceptance to work and live in the community.
- Cooperative leisure activities promote higher order communication and functional academic skills.

Basic Programme Principle

- Small interaction technique.
- Small group play with young retarded children.

- Provide an interdependent activity, which requires both individuals to participate.
- Pairing a mildly and severely retarded child together to promote social interaction.
- Using a more capable person with retardation to facilitate interaction.
- Teacher manually guides the students if they are not cooperating.
- Teacher as a participant motivates and involves the student to cooperate.

(e) Competition

Competition teaches students how to win and how to lose and provide a context for developing appropriate social behaviours, which many moderate and severely handicapped individuals are not at a competence level.

Competition has a limited rołe in leisure education programme for most moderately and severely handicapped individuals. However, with the influence of Special Olympics and other organized programmes we must be sensitive to this aspect of recreation.

Most recreational activities can be adapted to include either or both forms of competition.

By setting different "Winning" criteria according to each student's current level of performance, everyone is given the opportunity to be successful. Once the student has ample opportunities to experience success and failure in meeting some internal winning criteria, then direct competition can be introduced.

Role of Special Olympics

A major form of socialization in leisure for children with mental retardation is Special Olympics. As an internationally recognized recreation programme for persons with mental retardation, Special Olympics enjoyed participation. Thousands of mentally retarded children have competed in a variety of athletic activities since its inception in 1968. Special Olympics involve cooperative and competitive leisure activities throughout.

Advocates of Special Olympics feel that this programme allows for leisure participation by retarded children.

Various Aspects of Special Olympics

The benefits of participation in Special Olympics for people with mental retardation include improved physical fitness and motor skills, great self-confidence, a more positive self-image, friendships, and increased family support. Special Olympics athletes carry these benefits with them into their daily lives at home, in the classroom, on the job, and in the community. Families who participate become stronger as they learn a greater appreciation of their athlete's talents. Community volunteers find out what good friends the athletes can be. And everyone learns more about the capabilities of people with mental retardation.

The spirit of Special Olympics—skill, courage, sharing, and joy transcends boundaries of geography, nationality, political philosophy, gender, age, race or religion.

Special Olympics began in 1968 when Eunice Kennedy Shriver organized the First International Special Olympics Games at Soldier Field, Chicago, Illinois, USA. She saw that individuals with mental retardation were far more capable in sports and physical activities than many experts thought.

Around the world there are accredited Special Olympics programmes in more than 160 countries. Special Olympic Programmes are continually being developed around the world.

To be eligible to participate in Special Olympics, an athlete must be at least eight years old and identified by an agency or professional as having one of the following conditions: mental retardation, cognitive delays as measured by formal assessment which requires specially designed instruction.

The Special Olympics Unified Sports programme brings together athletes with and without mental retardation of similar age and ability to train and compete on the same teams. Founded in 1987, Special Olympics Unified Sports fosters the integration of persons with mental retardation into school and community sports programme.

Special Olympics provides year round training and competition in 25 official sports. Special Olympics has developed and tested training programmes that are outlined in a Sport Skills Guide for each sport. More than 140,000 qualified coaches train Special Olympics athletes.

By assigning athletes to divisions determined by their ages and ability levels, Special Olympics gives every athlete a reasonable chance to win. Athletes from all divisions may advance to State, National and World Games.

For athletes with profound disabilities Special Olympics created its Motor Activities Training Programme (MATP) developed by physical educators, physical therapists, and recreation therapists. MATP emphasizes training and participation rather than competition. MATP is part *of* the Special Olympics Commitment to offer sports training to an individual with mental retardation.

Special Olympics competitions are patterned after the Olympic games. More than 16,000 Games, meets and tournaments in both summer and winter sports are held worldwide each year, World Games for selected representatives of all programmes are held every two years, alternating between summer and winter.

Volunteers organize and run local Special Olympics programmes, serving as coaches, games officials, drivers and in many other capacities. Anyone can learn how to participate through the many training programmes Special Olympics offers for coaches, officials and volunteers.

Types of Sports

Special Olympics offers year-round training and competition in 25 Olympic-type sports to children and adults with mental retardation. Participation is open to anyone ages eight and up, and programmes are designed to serve all ability levels.

(a) Official Summer Sports

- Aquatics
- Athletics
- Basketball
- Bowling
- Cycling
- Equestrian sports
- Football (Soccer)

- Golf
- Gymnastics (Artistic and Rhythmic)
- Power lifting
- Roller Skating
- Softball
- Tennis
- Volleyball

Official Winter Sports

- Alpine Skiing
- Cross Country Skiing
- Figure Skating
- Floor Hockey
- Speed Skating

(b) Nationality Popular Sports

- Cricket
- Football
- Volleyball
- Kabbadi
- Badminton
- Table Tennis
- Team Handball

Training of Coaches

Coaches not only provide skills training for athletes but also serve as role models and character builders. They give Special Olympics athletes the most immediate awareness of their own worth, ability courage, and capacity to grow and improve.

Coaches fill a variety of different roles for Special Olympics programmes at the local, state, national and international levels. Coaches may include special education teachers, college students or family members of athletes, amateur and professional athletes and coaches, teachers and many others. A concerted effort also is made to target diverse individuals, including Special Olympics athletes who are interested in and capable of coaching. Special Olympics India trains athletes in one or more sports, including aquatics, athletics, badminton, basketball, cycling, football (soccer), team handball, volleyball and floor hockey.

Coaches also are instrumental in the development of Special Olympics, Unified Sports Programme. For instance, in Andhra Pradesh, unified sports in Football was held in 1977. The MATP is designed for lowest ability participants, who are unable to learn sports or compete. Unified sports is a program that brings together a proportionate number of persons with and without mental retardation and of similar age and ability to train and compete on the same team.

What Special Olympics Coaches Do?

- Assist athletes in learning sports skills.
- Encourage confidence and self-esteem through sports.
- Obtain equipment for athletic training.
- Conduct demonstrations in new sports.
- Start Special Olympics Unified Sports teams.

Special Olympics coaches often begin as volunteers at an event. In India, majority of the Coaches are staff member of special schools – being special education teachers or parent-teachers. Although no specific sport skill is required, many coaches already have expertise in the sports they select.

To become a certified Special Olympics coach, an individual must participate in a coach education course. The foundation course is the Special Olympics General Orientation, which offers information on Special Olympics as an organization and its uniqueness from other sport organizations, rules, mental retardation and eligibility. After deciding on a specific sport, the prospective coach attends a sport-specific skills course and completes a 10 hour practicum in training athletes. Upon completion, he or she is eligible for certification at the level. Special Olympics coaches often find they reap as many rewards from the training experience as do the athletes. Special Olympics coaches have a unique opportunity to work with athletes in competitive situations to assist in their training life.

Volunteers

Volunteers enable Special Olympics to offer sports training and competition programmes to more than one million individuals with mental retardation on a worldwide basis. Special Olympics would not exist today and could not have been created without the time, energy, dedication, and commitment of the more than 500,000 Special Olympics Volunteers.

Volunteers increase inclusion and socialization opportunities for Special Olympics athletes. The dedication of Special Olympics volunteers provides main streaming experiences for athletes with mental retardation.

Volunteers include college students, senior citizens, business people, family members of athletes, amateur and professional athletes and coaches, teachers and many others. They fill a wide variety of roles for Special Olympics programmes at the local, state, national and international levels, from the role of coach, to timer and scorers. In addition, Special Olympics athletes themselves provide an excellent source of volunteers.

Integration of Non-Handicapped Individuals

The first stage of integration can include the non-disabled children as volunteers within the actual Olympic events. They can be time-keeper, messenger, refreshment server, musician and coach.

The second level would involve disabled children as teachers during regular physical education classes at school. Retarded children could be taught by their peers to throw, run, jump and there by allowing individualized attention. This would facilitate more interaction between disabled and non-disabled children.

Very Special Arts (VSA)

The arts for the handicapped movement, which began in the 1970s attracted wide attention, along with the concept of Very Special Arts Festivals. The force behind this movement was the National Committee Arts for the Handicapped (NCAH), which emphasized the use of all arts in education. Very Special Arts was founded in 1974, by Kennedy Smith as an affiliate of the J. F. Kennedy Centre for Performing Arts in the US. It is now know as VSA Arts. VSA Arts India provides opportunities for children with mental retardation to receive training in visual and performing arts and exhibit their talents. Very Special Arts changed its name to VSA arts in 1999. VSA stands for Vision, Strength and Artistic Expression.

VSA India was founded in 1986 consisting of an Advisory Committee of prominent artists in the field of music, dance, drama and visual arts. Quality programmes in puppetry, weaving, painting, pottery, music, dance and drama are conducted throughout the year. It offers vocational training in arts, crafts and income generating programmes, such as weaving are gaining popularity. Once in a year, an All India Art Competition is held, where entries are invited from special schools, all over the country. The best exhibits are given cash awards and certificates. Selected works are printed as calendars and greeting cards.

Teacher training programmes are conducted at state level and national level in art education for persons with disability. The VSA National Festival is held once in 4 years, where children with disabilities are given opportunities to exhibit their talents and meet other artists. VSA encourage retired professionals, housewives, social workers and youth to give their time and skills, and benefits of their experience to the children with disabilities in order that they may be rehabilitated. These volunteers train children with disabilities to practice yoga, learn weaving, art, pottery and music, puppetry and dance.

A series of workshops on puppetry, art and craft and music and movement were held in a number of places in India sponsored by VSA 1996. Highlights of the workshop were innovative utilization of waste material, sample and clear ways of story telling and physical and voice exercises.

Abilympics

The International Abilympics Association was founded in 1981 by Mr. Harry Sang at Japan. Another well-known organization, which promotes the skills of people with disabilities is Abilympics Australia Association Inc. Its main objectives are:

- to encourage people with disabilities to take part in an active and constructive way by improving their vocational skills
- to demonstrate on an international level the standard of workmanship in open competition with other people with a disability of competing nations, where the quality of the work is the only item judged.
- to provide opportunities for people with disabilities to learn more about work skill opportunities through forums and seminars as well as networking with other disability organizations.

- there are 32 categories of events and two contestants from each country are allowed to participate. The assessment criterion is based solely on finished product. Special awards are given relating to the level of disability and efforts made. The awards granted are gold, silver and bronze medals, a certificate of merit and a citation for all participants.

The Indian Abilympics Association was instituted in the year 2000, and for the first time 14 contestants from India took part in the international event at Prague and won 10 gold medals. Of special mention is person with mental retardation who won a Bronze medal for Poster designing.

National Festival of Music and Dance

In the past, music and dance programmes for persons with mental retardation in our country has so far been limited to inter school cultural meets, competitions, regional and state/national level workshops for special teachers, in addition to VSA festival which is held once in four years. There has been no exclusive national programme where children with mental retardation could demonstrate their skills. Many exhibit extraordinary talent in music and dance. NIMH, in collaboration with Rajiv Gandhi National Institute of Youth Development, organized the National festival of Music and Dance for persons with mental retardation in the year 1999 at Secunderabad with the following objectives:

(i) To promote talents of persons with mental retardation.
(ii) To provide a common platform for them to see how others with similar conditions perform.
(iii) To extend the opportunity to trainers to exchange information.
(iv) To promote social and national integration.
(v) To provide access to persons with mental retardation with special talents to interact with celebrities in the field of music, dance and drama.
(vi) To create public awareness on the talents and creativity of persons with mental retardation.

Such festivals go a long way in promoting understanding in public about nature and needs of children with mental retardation, give them a chance to exhibit their creative abilities and bring about their social acceptance.

Very talented artists need to be encouraged by providing financial support for formal training in music and dance, which could serve as a vocation in future, leading towards their independent living.

Developing a Well-balanced Recreation Programme

In many schools, special Olympics is the major or even sole focus of the physical education programme for retarded students. It is questionable whether Special Olympics provides a vehicle for promoting independence and socialization. Its narrowness is especially apparent in children who have several physical and several interaction deficits. Is "throwing a softball" a meaningful activity to a girl with severe spastic quadriplegia? Does running the 100 feet dash permit a 16-year-old retarded boy as much independence and ability to interact with others? In short, the specific activities of the Special Olympics must be measured against the overall goals of the individual students.

Approaches to Integrated Recreation Services

There is a need for mentally retarded students to have access to a full range of physical and recreational activities with non-disabled peers.

1. *The Integration of Generic Recreation Programmes Approach*

In this approach an individual with severe disability selects a traditional, age appropriate recreation programme currently existing in the community. Then a professional with special training and a generic recreation programme personnel together work to include the person with disability to participate in the selected programme.

2. *Reverse Mainstreaming Approach*

In reverse mainstreaming, programmes designed for the people with disabilities are modified to attract non-disabled peers. This approach to recreation integration, which is practiced by the Special Olympics, is in its united sports programme.

3. *Creating a New Programme – The Zero Inclusion Approach*

In this approach, the specialists for disabled and non-disabled do not plan programmes in isolation. They collaborate to design the programmes for participation of both disabled and non-disabled.

Table-3: Pros and Cons of the 3 Approaches are given in the Diagram

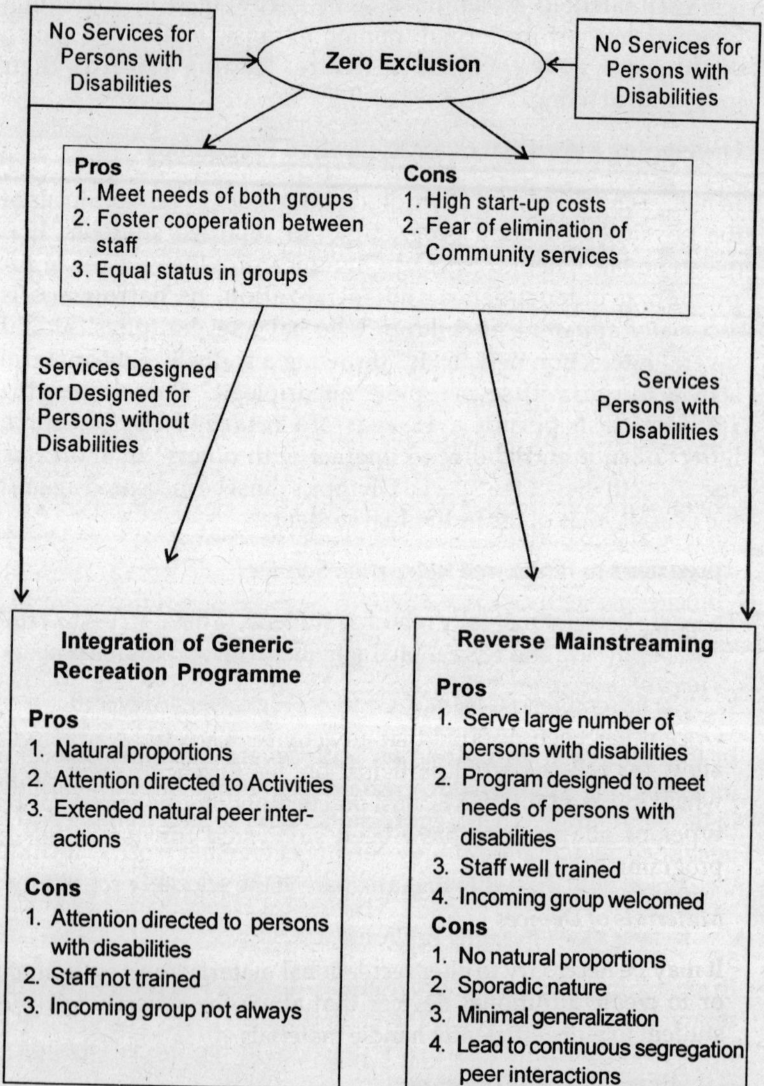

Snell, M.E. (1993), Instruction of Students with serve disabilities 4th edition– USA.

Best Professional Practices

Service providers choose from the strategies and tailor them to meet individual needs. Best professional practices include the following elements:

- Individual needs-assessments.
- Individual preference-assessment.
- Activity selection guidelines.
- Collateral skill development.
- Environmental analysis.
- Adaptations.
- Ability awareness on orientation and friendship training.
- Behavioural teaching method.
- Programme evaluation.

Adaptation Strategies

The Principle of Partial Participation

Even with adaptations some severely handicapped persons will not be able to participate independently in community based leisure programme. Even limited participation in an age-appropriate functional activity is more desirable than an independent segregated activity.

Types of Individual Adaptations

Once it has been decided that an activity needs to be adapted to allow for full or partial participation, the instructor must decide what kind of adaptation is most practical and normalizing. Various types of adaptations have been suggested for use in leisure programmes.

Materials of Devices

It may be necessary to alter recreational materials and equipments or to create additional devices that allow the severely retarded student to more efficiently handle materials.

Examples of adaptations:

Sports/fitness Activities

(i) Badminton	*Material*
	Short- handed racket
	Enlarged foam rubber racket handle
	Eliminate wind factor Lowered net Light- weight ball
(ii) Section 1.02 Basketball:	*Procedural/rules*
	More than 5 players (increase court coverage and eliminate need for long passes).
	Use of half a court Allow two hand dribbling Allow two or more stops per dribble.
(iii) Bowling	*Skill sequence*
	Trainer picks up ball and gives to bowler to perform a 'two handed' bowl.

Hobbies

Plant Care	–	Use 1 cup measure to prevent over watering
Cooking	–	Colour-code dials, picture recipies.
Needle work	–	Lacing board with plastic. Needle attached nylon cord Sewing cards to learn basic movements necessary for sewing.

Rule/Procedural Adaptations

Complicated rules and procedures can be extreme barriers to the participation of mentally and physically disabled in community-based leisure programmes, especially games and sports. Rules and procedures can be altered based on the severity level.

Environmental Adaptations

Persons with disability are denied participation in community based leisure programme due to inaccessibility of recreational facilities.

Narrow doors, lack of ramps and poorly designed toilet facilities are common problems. Other problems are lack of special equipments to aid in positioning, handling, and mobility of the multiple handicapped. The People with Disability Act (1995) mandates the construction of public facilities to include accessibility for the handicapped.

Skill Sequence Adaptation

The use of a task analysis is the best way to teach a leisure activity to severely retarded persons. However, the typical sequence of steps in a task analysis may have to be adapted for some individuals. For example, some steps may have to be done for the client or eliminated and others may need to be done in reverse order.

Unit Summary

The word leisure is derived from the Latin 'Licere' meaning to be free. This definition suggest not only that leisure time is free time but also that leisure activities must be freely chosen if they are to satisfy an individual's personal and social needs.

The characteristics of recreational and leisure programmes are fun and enjoyment, constructive or purposeful behaviour, participation and self-initiated behaviour and choice.

The individual education plans should reflect leisure objectives for acquisition and generalization of recreational skills.

The factors need to be considered for selecting leisure skills for instruction are chronological age-appropriations, attitude of parents and family members and attitude, aptitude and skills of the clients.

Various types of recreational and leisure activities have been classified into sports, games, hobbies and toy play. Some of the sports activities that can successfully be taught persons with mental retardation include individual exercises, playground activities, swimming, weight training and jogging.

Hobbies can involve sports, games, cooking, painting, observing and listening.

A comprehensive leisure education programme is complete only if it contains instruction for the development of independent leisure skills. Competition has a limited role in leisure education programme especially for moderately and severely handicapped individuals.

A major form of socialization in 'leisure' for children with mental retardation is Special Olympics. It involves cooperative and competitive leisure activity throughout.

Adaptations may include modification to components such as materials and equipments, rules of the activity, skill sequence and environment.

Yoga and very special arts are able to help persons with mental retardation recreational and leisure skills. There should be a repertoire of activities that can be taught and subsequently for which the materials are made available.

Role of mechanical use of one object for months and months is not the ultimate objective of a well-designed leisure programme.

Check Your Progress

- Define 'Leisure'.
- What are the characteristics of recreation and leisure programme.
- Explain the importance of leisure programme for persons with mental retardation.
- Discuss the approaches to integrated recreation services.
- Discuss the relevance of hobbies for children with mental retardation.
- Explain the basic principles involved in developing independent leisure.
- What do you mean by social instruction techniques?
- Examine the role of Special Olympics in the development of recreation and leisure time skills development.
- Discuss the need of adaptations in sports and fitness activities for persons with mental retardation.
- Explain the importance of yoga for children with mental retardation.
- Narrate the contributions of very special arts and Abilympics.

The criteria for selecting skills for leisure instruction are:

1.

2.

3.

Categories of leisure and recreational activities are:
Mention 2 – independent sports activities.
Mention 3 – team sports.
Name 3 – suitable hobbies for children with mental retardation.
Special Olympics was started in the year__________.
Make a list of 5 athletic items included in Special Olympics.

Assignment/Activities

Prepare the list of recreational activities which can be taught to persons with mental retardation at various levels

Points for Discussion/Clarification

....

....

....

....

REFERENCE

Brady, M.P., and Gunter, P.L. (1985), *Integrating Moderately and Severely Handicapped Learners*, Charles, C. Thomas, Publishers, USA Self-Instructional Material, B.Ed. Special Education, Bhoj Open University.